W9-AKT-528

Go happy hunting in the dating jungle . . .

Think about it. You're a modern, self-sufficient woman who makes her own choices and decisions. You go after what you want: job, lifestyle . . . so why not men? In *Get a Life, Then Get a Man*, Jennifer Bawden shows you how to

- Decide where to go, who to meet, how to take charge, initiate encounters, and make things happen
- Identify a man's "developmental" stages: the 20s, 30s, 40s—and how they affect who and what he's looking for
- Accept that you are not perfect
- Become more grounded in your goals
- Develop the kind of confidence that will draw people to you
- Master the art of female diplomacy
- Make a memorable first impression
- Make gracious exits
- Avoid unhealthy choices: Bad Boys, Someone Else's Husband, and Sugar Daddies
- Salvage a disaster date
- Recover from a broken heart
- Keep your options open

From setting objectives to nurturing friendships to being kind to yourself, this essential guide offers practical guidance and inspirational advice for every aspect of your life. You'll become the woman you always wanted to be—and meet fantastic men in the process!

Jennifer Bawden's fashion designs have been featured on the cover of *Cosmopolitan*, and have been worn by many celebrities, including Celine Dion, Mariah Carey, Ivana Trump, and Mariel Hemingway. She has been the recipient of Best New Talent Awards from Carolina Herrera, Dana Buchman, and the Fashion Institute of Design, and has been featured in magazines and newspapers including *Town and Country, Elle, The New York Times Magazine Fashion Supplement*, and *Condé Nast Traveler*. *Get a Life, Then Get a Man* is her first book.

Get a Life
Then
Get a Man

A Single Woman's Guide

Jennifer Bawden

A PLUME BOOK

PLUME
Published by the Penguin Group
Penguin Putnam Inc., 375 Hudson Street, New York, New York 10014, U.S.A.
Penguin Books Ltd, 27 Wrights Lane, London W8 5TZ, England
Penguin Books Australia Ltd, Ringwood, Victoria, Australia
Penguin Books Canada Ltd, 10 Alcorn Avenue, Toronto, Ontario, Canada M4V 3B2
Penguin Books (N.Z.) Ltd, 182–190 Wairau Road, Auckland 10, New Zealand

Penguin Books Ltd, Registered Offices: Harmondsworth, Middlesex, England

First published by Plume, a member of Penguin Putnam Inc.

First Printing, January, 2000
11 13 15 17 19 18 16 14 12

Copyright © Jennifer Bawden, 2000
All rights reserved

Ⓟ REGISTERED TRADEMARK—MARCA REGISTRADA

LIBRARY OF CONGRESS CATALOGING-IN-PUBLICATION DATA
Bawden, Jennifer
Get a life, then get a man: a single woman's guide / Jennifer Bawden.
p.   cm.
ISBN 0-452-28135-0
1. Single women—Conduct of life.   2. Self-realization.   3. Dating (Social customs)
4. Man-woman relationships.   I. Title.
HQ800.2.B39   2000
646.7'0086'52 21—dc21   99-045729

Printed in the United States of America
Set in Palatino
Designed by Leonard Telesca

Without limiting the rights under copyright reserved above, no part of this publication may be reproduced, stored in or introduced into a retrieval system, or transmitted, in any form, or by any means (electronic, mechanical, photocopying, recording, or otherwise), without the prior written permission of both the copyright owner and the above publisher of this book.

BOOKS ARE AVAILABLE AT QUANTITY DISCOUNTS WHEN USED TO PROMOTE PRODUCTS OR SERVICES. FOR INFORMATION PLEASE WRITE TO PREMIUM MARKETING DIVISION, PENGUIN PUTNAM INC., 375 HUDSON STREET, NEW YORK, NEW YORK 10014.

ACKNOWLEDGMENTS

I dedicate this book to my amazing family of friends who are the most important component of my life. Your love, support, enthusiasm, and belief in me have been the fuel for my continual metamorphosis on life's incredible journey. Oswald Bjelland, Dr. Adrian Denese, Bobbie Dupurton, Joanie and Sue Lennard, Sue Loranger, Sonja Pettingill, Albert Piacente, Leslie Vail, Allison Van Nest, Mike Weinstock, Alexandra Thilo, and, last but not least, my grandmother Sybil Grayburn, whose graciousness and kindness have always inspired me.

I also want to warmly thank the following people who generously shared their stories, wisdom, comments, criticism, or encouragement: Ann Doiron, Dick Levy, Alice Fasano, Sam Arcara, Louise Bresky, Mike Asante, Dawn Gallager, Jill Foote, Michelle Golden, Karen Gruber, Enid Haller, Robert Hochberg, Marnie Inskip, Rob Laidlaw, Tracy Mattikow, Andrew McKeon, Nancy Michula, John Norwood, Peter Schwartz, Ian Shapolsky, Randy Waterfield, Dr. Bridget Martel, Amanda Lang, Etienne Boillot, David Keisman, Leslie Barrett, Andrea Austin, Carol Sterbenz, and Stephen Warley.

Special thanks to Bob Leonard, Ken Leone, Nancy Romano, and my dear friends Andrea Ashford, Ed Rotter, Rich Lebuhn, and Randal Stempler for solving my seemingly endless computer problems.

Through the twenty-nine months it took me to complete this book, I had many assistants transcribe or type various drafts of this book. They not only worked endless hard hours with me, but their cheerful, warm, and positive demeanors made the time fun. I would especially like to thank: Karen Budham-Ali, Rachel Burward-Hoy, Pebbles Byndloss, Kristian Dietz, Yoon Jordan, Jenna Klatell, Jennifer Kushner, Kerissa

Rodrick, and Ann Swituszak. Most especially Katrina Green and Peggy Holguin who, with never a whimper, often worked the night or weekend shift to meet our deadlines.

I am also eternally grateful to Elsa Burt, Kate O'Brien Ahlers, and Sarah Demaree for their patience and persistence in editing different drafts of this manuscript.

Thanks to Steve Garrin for his incredible video-editing skills and to Sam Glenn, cameraman extraordinaire.

Thanks to Celine Dion, Andrea Bocelli, and Barbra Streisand, whose incredible voices kept me company during months of endless rewrites.

Special acknowledgment goes to Ron Nixon, for his creative ideas and unparalleled sense of humor; and to Camilla Rees for her wise counsel and steadfast commitment.

My heartfelt appreciation for their publicity skills goes to Rick Bard, Patti Cumming, Nancy Moon, Barb Tollis, Kim Murphy, Brant Janeway, Annie Jennings, Jay Severin, and the incredibly generous Jeff Jayson, mentor extraordinaire.

It would be impossible to find a better editor. I owe my greatest debt to Jennifer Dickerson Kasius at Plume, and my agent, Neeti Madan at Charlotte Sheedy/Sterling Lord Literistic, Inc. for believing in me.

Thank you everyone for being star players on my team.

CONTENTS

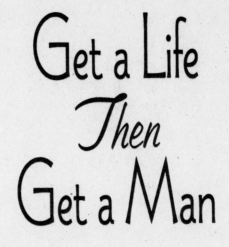

Get a Life
Then
Get a Man

Introduction

Boy meets girl. Boy likes girl but thinks girl doesn't like him. Actually, girl likes boy a lot, but she plays by the rules, pretending that she doesn't like him by playing hard to get. Boy gives up and looks elsewhere.

Have you read rule books that promote dating as a game and passivity as the winning strategy?

Did you: (a) laugh and toss your rule books down the toilet; (b) see red and throw them across the room; or (c) cry and hide them under your pillow, just in case?

Are you—or would you like to be—a strong, independent, confident woman in charge of her own life, one who isn't afraid to go after what she wants?

Are you sick of feeling that aspiring to be any of the above makes you unattractive to men?

Do you detest game-playing and dishonesty?

If you answered yes to any of the above, then welcome! You're not alone—and take heart, because someone has finally written a book for *you!*

* * *

Books teaching women to be looks-obsessed, passive, or untrue to their real feelings in order to catch a man imply that our real, amazing selves are simply not good enough—or somehow too much to handle and we must therefore pretend to be someone we're not. I want to offer an alternative to women who have worked toward independence and achieve-ment and who believe it's possible to apply sensible, straight-forward strategies in the search for a lifetime partner.

I came to New York City from Canada without knowing a soul, so I know how tough it can be to meet new people. But with perseverance, I navigated the crowd, built my own fash-ion business, formed a strong group of girlfriends, and met many of the world's most interesting and exciting men. My unconventional, proactive approach to meeting people pro-duced rapid-fire results and greatly enriched my life. I let my girlfriends in on my approach, and the ones who adopted these proactive techniques have met and built relationships with dynamic, loving men—including CEOs, doctors, invest-ment bankers, artists, TV producers, even real-life princes. As a direct result of my tactics, thirty-five of my friends found their husband, wife, or fiancé.

The Past

There was a time when society gave power and importance to men automatically. They ran the institutions and made the rules and the important decisions. Women adapted to their environment and conditions. We were, for the most part, con-fined at home. We were "shopped around" by a suitable chap-erone, and then we waited for men to drop off their calling cards. We dated and most often married the men our families (usually our fathers) had chosen. We married young or earned the dreaded title of "spinster."

Passive attitudes may be acceptable to those who believe they can't have a man and their own dreams simultaneously and so give up their personality and desires to let the man run the show. But is that who you are? Perhaps if you follow the passive approach, a man will eventually come along. But what kind of man will he be? Probably one who wants to make all the decisions for his meek and mild mate.

The Present

Well, thank goodness, times have changed. Women today have more freedom and more opportunities to make better choices than ever before. We have fought for the right to be active and equal in every facet of our lives. Why then, as we launch into the twenty-first century, should we accept the notion that we must remain passive to get a mate? Why should we only choose from the men who approach, call, or "drop off their calling cards"? Why can't we pursue the men we want just as we have learned to pursue our careers and goals? Is it simply because we live with traditions passed down by women who were not as liberated as we are? What would our ancestors have said about sharing the workplace with men? Making the same amount of money as men? What about a woman buying her own home?

In researching this book, I talked to a great many men, most of whom have grown up in this new era. Many of their mothers worked. They have been surrounded by smart, independent women who are not afraid to pursue what they want. They've encountered women in the corporate ranks as role models, mentors, and bosses. These men want women primed for the future and everything it has to offer, not a woman who plays hard to get. They are attracted to independent women with their own lives. As my friend Mike, a successful twenty-six-year-old district attorney, says, "I can give her companionship and love, but I have enough trouble taking care of myself. The last thing I need is the responsibility of taking care of someone who's a clingy dependent." Don't get stuck in the Stone Age. Remember, men have also formed new sensibilities for love, long-term relationships, and marriage.

The Future

Too many women are still expecting a man to make the first move. No more! Take matters into your own hands and reclaim your power. This book will help you decide exactly what kind of man is right for you and show you how to develop the confidence to attract him. You will learn how to enter a room or a party, decide who you would like to meet, and engage that man in conversation. This book will *not* teach you how to manipulate a man or conceal your real self in order to snag a husband. Instead, it will show you how to take a proactive rather than a reactive role in choosing a compatible partner who shares your vision of a happy, honest, meaningful life. (After all, the goal here is to find a man who loves you because of who you really are.) Most important, you will learn how to make the right choices and set high standards for yourself and the men you choose. Now don't be scared. I'm not advocating running after him like a hungry animal—there's a right way and a wrong way, of course. But trust me, when you know how to approach a man with genuine, friendly interest, not only will he be relieved, but he'll be flattered you chose him. And you'll be well on your way to having more dates than you ever dreamed of and finding "Mr. Right." This book outlines a surefire strategy that works, as all of my now married friends who met their significant others following this philosophy will attest.

It's time to stop helplessly waiting to be some man's prey and start thinking like a sophisticated huntress. Which leads me to . . .

Empowerment

Attractive, intelligent women are sitting at home right now waiting for the phone to ring. I believe you deserve to go out and get what you want. Not just a man, but whatever else you want. Being proactive in your life means reaching your highest potential. Women who follow the old rules are looking for men to save them. Unsure how to reach their goals, afraid of hard work, failure, or even success, they will never reach their goals or develop their own strong life. If women spent half the time they waste worrying about dating, clothes, and makeup and used that time to develop themselves, they would be happier and more successful, and they'd attract the men they want. What is *your* destiny? Your destination? It isn't enough to just think about it—you need to make it happen. This book will show you how. Work on yourself and your goals first, and the right man will follow. I guarantee it.

For these reasons, the first few chapters are about taking stock of yourself and your life, working through your concerns, and preparing yourself for a long-term meaningful relationship. Wouldn't you like, first and foremost, to be a confident, well-rounded woman? When you know who you are and what your goals and dreams are, you can find a man who understands and respects them. And if you haven't resolved your own inner conflicts, how are you going to believe deep down that you really deserve this wonderful man?

This book is about the whole you, about enhancing every aspect of your life, since it's almost impossible to have a healthy relationship without first loving and understanding yourself. This book will show you how to invest in your own growth and self-confidence, so that whatever choices you make—whether they concern your life, career, or relationships—will be the right ones. Empowerment is the key. Waiting for your metaphorical ship to come in will leave you stranded on dry land. So roll up your sleeves and get ready to do some real work so you can be the very best that you can be.

And while we're on the subject of being in control of your own life . . .

Make Your Own Damn Rules!

First of all, this is not a rule book. It's a guidebook. Like a map, it will simply point out new directions and ways to connect with yourself, your personal goals, and ultimately, if you choose, with a fantastic man.

Listen to what your body, heart, soul, and mind are telling you about who you are and who you can be. Decisions made from this sacred place will take you where you need to go. More than anything, I want to help you discover your own inner rules, to listen to your own inner wisdom about what and who is really going to bring you happiness, growth, and fulfillment.

As our busy lives overwhelm us, we often tune out this intuitive voice. But true fulfillment is found by listening carefully and hearing what this inner voice has to say. This method has worked for me. If you let it, the lessons you learn will touch your life, sharpen your focus, and remind you of instincts that you've felt all along. Of course, I don't expect you to agree with everything. My advice will apply to some situations but not to all. Use your own reason, trust your intuition and enjoy the advice that speaks to you!

Oh, and one last thing; for goodness' sake . . .

Break Out of the Spinster Funk!

Many women feel incomplete without a guy in the picture. They put themselves under a lot of pressure to find a man. As a result, meeting men ceases to be fun. It becomes an obsession, an almost desperate, dreaded chore.

When I feel the funk closing in like a foggy day, I remind myself of all the benefits of being single: I can make my own decisions quickly. I'm free to do whatever I want, whenever I want. I don't have to consider anyone's objections. And I'm not depending on someone else for my happiness. When I'm single, new situations arise, life is less routine, and I have more time to learn about myself and to figure out what I like and don't like. And there's more time to spend with my friends. Appreciate the spontaneity and freedoms of being single.

Our society is obsessed with having it all right now. Why not try enjoying what you already have? What's your rush? Relax; celebrate being single. Don't put so much pressure on yourself to achieve the prescribed end result of man/boyfriend/marriage. This is your time, so make the most of it. Use it to make yourself a more educated, interesting person with a full life of your own. Savor and enjoy this wonderful, carefree, fun time. Be comfortable alone. Remember: A man is not the solution. You are.

Katie knew she just needed a little help to get her going. Something to get her onto the "Path to Unimaginable Treasures." She held two books in her hand. Opening the first she saw it was full of rules on how to trick and trap a man into marriage. "Aargh," she exclaimed, frightening a few purse-lipped women nearby clutching their own rule books. She tossed the book into the nearest trash can and opened the second book, which was full instead, thankfully, of powerful inspiration and steps on how to take action. Katie looked up, saw her Path, and began to walk, flashing a brilliant smile.

PART I

Get a Life

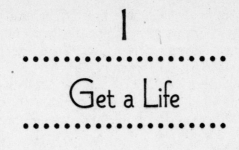

Get a Life

Katie sat patiently on the loveseat, looking out the tower window. Occasionally, she thought she could see him in the distance, his strong white horse beneath him, his long, dark hair flowing, coming closer, coming for her, but then the vision would fade away.

Before you turn your thoughts to finding a man, focus on developing your goals and your friendships. Think of the couples you most admire who seem to enjoy and support each other. Most likely they have their own unique interests and ambitions. Many women waste time on the wrong man because of a desperate need for companionship. Often they mistake a feeling of togetherness for that of true love. If you are happy and satisfied with your life, you'll attract quality men with similar values. Enter relationships from a full, satisfied place, not a lonely one.

Amanda has more sex appeal than any other woman I know. Men trip over themselves to meet and spend time with her. Headhunters constantly call, offering positions of greater responsibility. Her allure is her confidence, independence, and strong sense of self-respect. Busy with her fulfilling life, men instinctively feel she won't pressure them for a commitment.

Rather, they know they will have to entice her into a relationship, by being at least as interesting as the many other aspects of her life. Amanda commands respect. What better position is there from which to begin a relationship?

When I arrived in New York, I only had the bare essentials: two friends, their fold-out couch for a month, and a college degree. I knew that to build and maintain a solid foundation in this town was going to be a challenge and take a lot of discipline. But I also knew I didn't want to wake up years later thinking, "This isn't the life I wanted. This isn't who I wanted to be." Naïve and idealistic, I was determined to work toward my dreams and somehow make a difference in this city.

These are the eight steps I took to create a new, exciting, fulfilling, and successful life.

Step One: Start Developing a Life Plan

A sense of purpose—knowing what you want—is paramount to building a strong foundation. For my first few months in the city I wandered aimlessly, overwhelmed by the excitement and opportunities. Things were happening so quickly that it was all I could do to just react without ever thinking about how I was allocating my time. I needed to develop a plan. People prepare business plans for their companies. I thought, Why not do one for myself? What should I do? How could I create greater meaning in my life? I seriously examined what I wanted from life. Was it to have money? To make a difference in people's lives? To have fun? To grow in love and compassion? To have children? What is my mission? If someone asked me who I was, what would I tell them? What are you passionate about? Looking back, what would I like my life to have meant? Answering these questions provided me with a strong motivation to help me reach my goals. Writing them down on paper immediately made me feel so much more focused. Knowing which highway to take is key to arriving at your destination.

Make your own goal list. Ask yourself what you've always wanted to do, to learn, to be? Listen to your deepest desires. Dare to express your own uniqueness. Do you want to continue your education? Did you always want to learn to play the piano or wish you could sing professionally? Would you like to learn to speak French? How about taking up mountain climbing? Remember, nothing is too outrageous—write them all down. Think back to your school days. What was your favorite subject? At what did you excel? Ask your friends or family or talk to former teachers. If you're having trouble coming up with ideas, check out career centers that analyze your personality and skills and give professional suggestions. Try your high school or college career center. They often allow alumni to use their facilities.

Now, take this list and break it down. First of all, create a realistic, achievable list of the things you wish to accomplish, and then divide them into short- and long-term objectives. This is the "life list" from which you will work. Make a second list of everything you'd like to do if your wildest dreams could come true. Label this your "fantasy list." Don't throw away these lists—in a short time you'll realize these goals and fantasies are more accessible than you ever imagined! These pieces of passion and seemingly wild ideas will often come into focus.

A life list sets the targets, dreams, goals and ambitions of your life. Your goals might be:

Run a marathon
Visit Australia
Get my own apartment
Learn to speak Spanish
Take scuba diving lessons
Write a book
Go to cooking school
Learn to play the piano

* * *

Writing down my goals was one of the most important and useful exercises I ever did. It gave my life a clear direction and meaning. Your own list should be reexamined and revised often throughout your life, either to help you stay on track or to make revisions when you change your goals. If you feel overwhelmed, make a list of your short-term goals only, and build on these.

Step Two: Get Organized

I learned the hard way that chaos ensued unless I was organized. Until I made the commitment to get organized, important opportunities fell through the cracks. I spent tremendous energy navigating through the chaos rather than establishing priorities and focusing on my goals. My most embarrassing moment, that resulted from my disorganization was when the doorbell rang half an hour early and to my surprise it wasn't the date I expected. I had inadvertently scheduled two dates for the same night. I frantically tried to call the second date to explain. He'd already left work and was on his way to pick me up. This nauseous feeling swept over me and my heart raced. I decided to take the high road. When both arrived I sat them down and said, "I'm sure you're wondering why you're both here and are feeling a bit uncomfortable, but I want you to know I'm more uncomfortable than you could both possibly be." I then told them the truth apologizing profusely. They both had a great sense of humor and suggested we all go out together. This story has gotten a lot of mileage and the two guys, great friends today, still laugh over how they met. Learn from my mistakes; here's how to keep your sanity.

Start a To Do List

Keep it handy and add things to the list as they come up. When you complete something on the list, put a line through it. Color coding works well. For example, underline in black what you would like to accomplish on Monday. Then at the end of the day underline Tuesday's goals in red. Have a spot to remind yourself of calls to make. Keep it as neat as possible. Every Sunday I redo my list, so I'm organized and clear for the following week.

Create Your Own Mini Yellow Pages

I keep a wealth of useful information in the back of my personal phone book. For instance, there's a section for hotels, restaurants, places to dance, places I like to go, moving companies, piano players, photomats, art supplies, etc. Through the years, I've collected a great list of resources. If you choose to keep this on your computer, make sure to keep a backup disk, and *never* let your primary phone book out of your house. Make a copy of it and carry around with you a small book with frequently used numbers.

Prioritize

Spend some time going through every loose piece of paper you own and put them into one of three piles: Urgent, Soon, and Rainy Day. I use large Ziploc bags to hold the sorted papers. Files or large envelopes also work. Keep the Soon and Rainy Day piles handy, but put your Urgent pile prominently on your desk or bedside table. Every week, I take out the most important projects and put them on top of my To Do list. My goal is to get through the pile I've set for myself.

Help Yourself

Think about how you can conserve time. Try to do all of your grocery shopping in one weekly trip or trade off chores with friends. You could alternate walking your dogs or create a car pool. If you can afford it, consider hiring someone to help you get some of the time-consuming errands done so you can focus on your To Do list.

Declutter

There are certain things I hate to do or find incredibly boring, such as paying the bills or filing. To make the best use of my time and to help the time fly by, I do them while watching my favorite TV shows or listening to great music. Go through and organize the piles you've accumulated and throw out anything you don't need. A clutter-free environment inspires calmness and a sense of progress.

Step Three: Knowledge Is Power

It's great to have goals, but without knowing how to go after them, you won't get very far. To prepare for the future, learn about the areas you want to explore. Find out as much as you can via the Internet, your public library, magazines, or books. Talk to as many people as possible who are involved in your areas of interest. Try nearby schools. Make appointments with teachers or professionals in the career you may choose. Ask questions. Most people are willing to give advice. Listen to critical suggestions but don't let anyone discourage your dreams. Someone told me, "Forget it. It's so hard to be a fashion designer." Instead of letting this stop me, I focused on finding positive people and role models who were busy reaching their own goals and were supportive of mine.

Find out about courses offered at local schools. Colleges and technical schools offer weekend or night classes for people who work. With a little diligence, you can uncover thousands of independent scholarship funds for every field through your local library or the Internet. You may also find government alternatives to financing your studies. Many colleges have special women's support groups that provide free counseling. Just ask. Education isn't a way to keep busy while waiting for marriage. Rather, it's a stepping stone to making your life more complete.

Setting goals is like planting a garden. You'll plant seeds a long time before the garden grows. Start planting those seeds! There are lots of opportunities out there. Research them, decide which ones interest you, and turn them into reality.

Step Four: Believe Your Instincts

"If you can dream it you can do it."

—Walt Disney

For Kathy, a very talented artist, her own thoughts were her worst enemy. She created more self-doubt and put up more imagined roadblocks than existed in reality. As she listened to voices in her subconscious that told her "You can't do that! An exhibition? Yeah? Right!" she finally acknowledged she was holding *herself* back. "I was just sick of feeling like a loser. I finally realized I had as much a right as anyone to reach my potential." She committed to make an effort to catch and switch every negative thought to a positive one. "Every night before I went to bed and every morning when I woke up, I said 'I am a great artist' ten times. The old programming was saying no, I wasn't special. I chose yes!"

It took extreme concentration and focus to notice when she was being negative. "At first it was really hard to focus on the positive; soon, it actually became natural." Kathy is the source of her own power and potential. Connecting with her confidence and her passion was much more important than her circumstances. "I thought as a young artist I wasn't good enough for a show, let alone a gallery." By writing down and reviewing her negative self-beliefs at the end of each week she could ask herself, "Where did this thought come from? How can I change it?" Within two months it was clear to everyone who knew her that a transformation had taken place. Kathy put together a slide show of her work and had signed a deal with a top gallery downtown. "The only thing wrong with my paintings was that I didn't believe they were good enough."

Imagine yourself reaching your goal: What does it feel like?

How has it affected your life? Hold on to your vision, and know you can achieve it. Don't let anyone—especially yourself—ever stop you. There is no limit to how far you can go and what you can accomplish. Almost anything is possible. Believe it.

My greatest passion has always been to sing. As a teenager, looking to others for validation, I was discouraged by the cynical critiques of a few friends. This stunted my ambition and sense of my own potential. Afraid I had no chance of ever succeeding, I let this dream go. Eventually, confident in other aspects of my life, I finally enrolled in singing lessons. When I realized I was replaying the old criticism of years ago, I changed my tune to "I have a great voice." Since then, with hours of practice my voice has blossomed. This belief in my potential came through loud and clear and my voice dramatically improved.

Step Five: Focus

Now you have identified your personal goals and cut out the inconsequential things that waste your time and distract you from achieving them. It's time to make a difference. Exercise your own free will. Create and envision the reality you want and commit to making it happen. If you have time to watch TV or wait by the phone for a man to call, then you have time to start learning and moving toward your goals. Make this and every day count. Your life is too important not to.

If I wanted to succeed in the notoriously competitive Big Apple, I knew that I would need to give whatever it took to get the job done. This meant staying up working many nights until 2:00 A.M. It meant being more selective and eliminating some of the parties, people, or pastimes (like television) that distracted me from accomplishing my goals. Most important, it meant making a deep commitment to myself to follow through one step at a time. Every hour brought me that much closer. A friend told me she wanted to write a book, but that her busy doctor's schedule kept her from focusing on this dream. I suggested that instead of tackling the whole book, she commit to one page a day. In nine months, she had it finished! All it took was a small, consistent, devoted effort.

Step Six: Activate Yourself

Another friend of mine remarked, "Every day my sister sits around and talks about what she wants to do. Yet she continues in the same pattern: going to her job, coming home, eating dinner, watching television, and going to bed." Just sitting at home and talking about it won't get you anywhere. But with a small step every day you will be singing those songs, playing that piano, designing those clothes, and achieving anything else you want. Small, consistent efforts make a big difference over the long haul. By taking action you *will* transform your life.

I wasn't prepared to leave things to chance. I knew I had to go out and make them happen. Stake my claim in the world. Challenge yourself to take bold initiatives and stride toward the goals on your own life list. Yes, this means breaking out of your comfort zone to expand your horizons, but the results will be tremendous!

Start by breaking down your goals into small, simple steps. Tackle them one at a time. Here are the steps I followed in my goal to become a fashion designer:

- Learn pattern-making/draping and figure drawing.
- Thoroughly research the dress market.
- Work for a fashion company as an assistant designer.
- Create my own line of dresses.
- Show my dresses to top stores' buyers (I made a hit list of exactly which stores).
- Take my dresses to the editors of all relevant magazines.

To get to the future you envision, look at your goal list every single day (try sticking it on your mirror—in large type!) and do something toward one of those goals. Ask yourself, "What am I going to tackle today?" If one of your goals is to learn how to sing, make a call to the local music school and ask for a catalog for evening or weekend classes. I did this and was shocked to find out that even top schools like Juilliard had night classes that accepted me. Get the materials you need. Buy the self-teaching book, the language tape, French books, sign up for riding lessons, buy those running shoes, etc. Keep busy doing. Move forward every day, and over the course of a year or two, when you look back, you'll have accomplished a lot. You'll have learned and grown. You win either way. Even if you haven't yet reached your goals, you're way ahead of where you started. And the journey will have been fun, exciting, and challenging.

To begin, put on your favorite music for inspiration, then make a commitment. "Today I am going to kick up my heels, and take steps to change my life." When you start pursuing the life you want, you'll automatically start feeling better about yourself. Don't be threatened by possibility—thrive on it!

Step Seven: Surround Yourself with Positive People

> "To be nobody but yourself in a world which is doing its best, night and day, to make you 'everybody else' means to fight the hardest battle which any human being can fight, and never stop fighting."
>
> —e. e. cummings

Now that you believe in your ability, you'll need to surround yourself with positive, supportive people who encourage you. There is no place for unfounded cynicism from family, friends, or lovers who don't believe in your potential. It will only hold you back. Imagine how much happier and easier your journey will be with positive people around you.

Every few months I organize a girls' dinner, inviting only the girlfriends who inspire and support me. No exceptions.

They share their goals and I share mine. When you know what your friends hope to accomplish, you can offer additional support by clipping articles, sharing contacts, and offering encouragement.

Keep in mind that some friends or family members may feel threatened. Your new direction may make them look at themselves and remind them they're not moving forward in their own lives. Your new ideas and drive demand change, and this can be threatening or frightening. Don't let them drag you down. Beware of well-meaning "elders" offering advice that will hold you back. They may not believe you can reach your dreams, and, afraid that you will fall or be hurt, they may discourage you. Hear their fears, but trust your heart. Decipher what's relevant but always come back to your deep sense of knowing what's right for yourself.

Learning to tune out these negative voices can be difficult, because everyone has been socialized to care about what others think. So we listen and believe the pessimism of others. Some may be valid; however, others can just as easily stifle as empower you. These put-downs or concerns often reveal their own limitations, not yours. They're projecting their own inadequacies. Observe everyone around you. Are they negative influences or do they offer positive advice and encouragement? Even if it hurts their feelings, let the negative people know, "I'm making some changes in my life and I need people who are positive and supportive around me." Don't let them constantly put down your ideas and dreams. It's difficult enough staying motivated and focused without the people close to you bringing you down. They won't like this, but you must make yourself clear. "Support me and be positive, because I'll be spending most of my time with people who do." Then follow through. Hopefully they will quickly change their tune. Meanwhile, allow skepticism or pessimism to inspire you. Show them it *can* be done!

When I left Toronto, my dear paternal grandmother (who always had my best interests at heart) felt compelled to tell me, "You're behaving like Alice in Wonderland. If you actually think anybody in New York will buy a dress you've designed, you're crazy!" Within four years, I had my dresses on six *Cosmopolitan* covers and in the Fifth Avenue windows of Bergdorf Goodman. So here's my answer to the naysayers: "Just because you think *you* can't do it doesn't mean *I* can't do it!" I told my grandmother that if she wasn't going to support my goals, I would stop telling her about them. I explained that I needed all the strength and encouragement I could muster to accomplish them. From then on, our relationship grew into one of respect and encouragement. I loved her, but by letting her know I wouldn't accept her negativity, she learned to keep those thoughts to herself. Instead of being an anchor, she let me sail.

Has anyone ever told you that you were nobody special? Have they said you shouldn't try to reach the stars or make a difference? Refuse to believe them. Take a stand and stop allowing others (or yourself) to hold you back. Don't let fear, or what anybody else thinks, stop you from winning. If you hide what you want because it's unacceptable to your mate, family, or friends, you're never going to feel fulfilled. In a healthy relationship, people cultivate their own goals. Don't be afraid to achieve because you think it will intimidate those around you. They are more likely to stay with you when you're doing something interesting, challenging, and new. Growth is always more exciting than staying the same. Take control of your own life. You can do it!

Step Eight: Enjoy the Journey

Enjoying the scenery every step of your climb is as important as reaching the top and feeling the exhilaration of accomplishing a goal. Live your dream every day. Be happy and proud you're doing what you choose. Acknowledge that you're happy just moving forward. Don't postpone happiness until you reach your goal.

I've heard many women complain, "I'm so tired of working. I just want to find a guy so I can get married and settle down." This might seem like a logical solution, but if they were doing something that they loved, they wouldn't be tired. They'd wake up every day wanting to start their day. Instead of finding a man to save you from your job, find work that you're passionate about. At least try to find one element of your job that inspires you.

Resist your impulse to say, "Oh, I could never quit my job." A dead-end job that makes you miserable will never lead anywhere. You can't give your all to something you don't believe in. And it's crazy to think you should suffer at a job you hate. Don't accept it as part of life. Who told you that you were born to suffer?

Your deeper longings can only be satisfied by working toward—and reaching—your goals. If you can't change your work, remember to fill the rest of your life with achievements you do love. Too often, we spend so much time—more time than needed or expected—worrying about the company's objectives. Keep a healthy balance and don't let an unsatisfying job make you miserable. Live for more than a paycheck. The fulfillment of doing what you love is a great reward in itself. Your soul is worth nurturing. Your life is worth enjoying.

Anne-Marie, unhappily married and tired of her job selling business forms, complained, "My life has been dull for years. It's time to start living again. I want to be more, I want to do more, I want to enjoy life. I want to have a bounce in my step when I go to work. I'm bored at my job. I want out." She finally acknowledged her spirit wasn't aligned with her career, which prevented her from expressing her creativity. She had clipped an article out of *Forbes* magazine on career coaching. She actually found a site on the Internet called "Coach University" [www.coachu.com], where she located a counselor who could help her navigate a career transition. The coach had worked in advertising and knew exactly where to lead her. She directed Anne-Marie to headhunters in advertising and finally she secured a job she loves as an account executive. This fresh start made all the difference in salvaging her marriage. Happy with herself, she finally had more to give to her family.

Regardless of whether you are single or happily (or unhappily) married, it's essential to take steps toward creating a life and a job you enjoy. No matter how stuck you feel in your current job or life situation, realize you're only one proactive step away from getting on track toward a goal, and the tremendous excitement that comes with it. Once you break through the mental barrier and take the first few steps you'll find all kinds of resources to support you that you might not even know exist.

Dealing with Setbacks

"Explore all possibilities available, never shrink back from any challenge, rush to it, welcome it, rise to the occasion— then life becomes a flame, life blooms. See every difficulty as a challenge, a stepping stone, and never be defeated by anything or anyone."

—Eileen Caddy

It would be crazy to pretend it's all easy sailing. I know I've encountered lots of problems along the way. In fact, there were times when I wanted to quit. Here are five additional steps I used when I felt like bailing. They helped me stay on course and overcome the hurdles. After all, knowing how to confront and handle setbacks is perhaps the most important part in achieving success. In fact, there were many times when a setback ultimately guided me closer to my goals. Above all, remember that the strength you need flows from within you.

Step One: Change Your Outlook

Life is always going to be full of difficulties. It may be a small setback or a mountain standing in your way. Try to see both the good, happy days and the frustrating, difficult times as just different lessons in the school of life! Life is in constant flux, and problems are part of our daily experience. Know and accept this. It helps to look at your goals as puzzles to put together. Like the Sunday crossword, life becomes fun and challenging. As every new problem comes along in your journey, don't get angry. Expect it. Know that you can solve it, change it, adapt to it, modify it, and overcome it.

Don't allow yourself to get stuck in the "woe is me" mentality. Contentment comes when you ride over the bumps with the same calm disposition as during the clear, easy stretches. Embrace unpredictability. "Oh, another bump, I've been expecting you." Solutions can often emerge simply by cultivating a calm mindset amidst chaos. With this attitude, you won't sit back and say, "The world is against me." Instead, you'll proudly say, "I had five problems today, I solved four of them. Tomorrow I'll work on solving the fifth, and I'll be that much closer to realizing my goal." True success is finding fulfillment in everyday struggles.

Somehow, Joanne got the notion that life should be easy. Every week she had a different excuse for postponing her happiness. "If only my transfer would come through, I could get away from this job and these miserable people. Then my life would be simple, and I'd be happy." Nobody has a problem-free life. Problems are part of the human process. "If I only had money, I'd be happy." Many wealthy people aren't at all happy. "If only I were married, I'd be happy." Wrong again. Happiness doesn't come from acquiring something or someone, it comes from within you. Joanne's greatest reward or achievement in life is neither the dollars earned nor the husband married, but how she's grown and been transformed by her experiences.

Every failure taught me much more than each success. When I tried to get my dresses into the magazines I had to deal with many rejections. There were thousands of young designers and only limited magazine space. All my friends were buying and wearing my dresses and I was confident there would be a demand if I could only get them to the public. I wasn't going to take no for an answer; I knew there had to be a way in. As I researched the decision-making process I found out the photographers yield quite a lot of power and with a few more meetings landed my dresses on the covers instead. Every mistake or rejection leads to a revelation. By understanding what wouldn't work, I learned what could.

Every time I traveled outside my comfort zone, I grew more confident, understanding and empathetic to others in the same position. I had to change my attitude and not let problems take me by surprise. This meant turning negatives into positives by seeing each setback as an opportunity. Sometimes this became apparent months or even years later. For example, when I decided to have my debut party as a designer, I organized a huge fashion show for all the top press and store buyers. After weeks of my hard work, the venue had to cancel all events. I was thunderstruck. But months later, the factory I would have been working with filed for bankruptcy. When I couldn't deliver my dresses to the stores in time I would have lost credibility and my money would have been tied up in unfinished goods. In retrospect, I was extremely thankful that my fashion show had been canceled. From then on I took disappointments much more in stride.

Step Two: Focus on Solutions

Worrying has never solved a problem. It's like losing your keys at home and freaking out. They always show up, and all you accomplished was to make yourself crazy. Instead of wasting time blaming others or complaining, use your skills and energy to find a solution! Solve the problem. Otherwise you're letting the circumstances of life rule you. By taking action, moving the rocks in your path one by one, you can rearrange things so your life works for you. Sometimes the pile seems daunting. The secret is to keep returning to remove another rock. Even if you're afraid, the only way to find a solution is to face your problem head-on.

Step Three: Be Persistent

*"Nothing in the world can take the place of persistence.
Talent will not; nothing is more common than unsuccessful
men with talent. Genius will not; unrewarded genius is
almost a proverb. Education will not; the world is full of
educated derelicts. Persistence and determination alone
are omnipotent."*

—Calvin Coolidge

Life can be like moving through a swamp. Sometimes
there's no land in sight, just swamp snakes, buzzards, croco-
diles and quicksand that's dragging you down fast. This is
when you develop "character." Don't give up, not even when
you feel the quicksand about to move over your ears. Slowly,
one inch at a time, work your way to dry land. Even if you
can't see it, visualize it. Believe me, you'll make it. Yes, it can
be a challenge—the challenge of your life—but it's worth it.
You're worth it.

Many talented people avoid entering the competition. You
too can stay in your safety zone, away from risk, far away from
the swamp, but you'll never be able to stand on the other side
of that swamp, on dry ground, successful and proud of what
you've accomplished. And, most important, if you don't wade
through it or put yourself up to the challenge, you'll never
have that feeling, that knowledge, that if you set your mind to
it, you can accomplish anything.

In high school, I loved to ski and was determined to compete. I fell a hundred times and thought that I would never be
in the same league with the other competitors. But instead of
focusing on how talented the other skiers were, I concentrated
on improving my own speed and technique. The day of the
provincials came, I was happy just to be included. To my complete shock I took home a silver and a bronze medal in two
events! When you only try to win, you lose sight of the goal:
being the best you can be.

Of course, it's only natural for your feelings to change when

you're in a tough spot. You might lose heart, but your commitment to realizing your goals must stay constant. Some days, I
felt happy and excited with my progress. Other days were difficult. I felt lazy, tired, frustrated, or disappointed. It doesn't
matter what you feel day to day. The only thing that matters is
that you keep coming back to the goal. You may slip off your
diet for a day or two or even a week. But if you stick with it
you'll shed those pounds. One fall, or even a hundred, doesn't
equal failure. I program and reinforce my daily commitment
every morning when I get up. Be clear: "Today I am working
on X and Y." No matter what the daily setbacks, no matter how
deep the swamp, hold your dreams in your mind and heart.

Connecting with your vision as you fall off to sleep rein-
forces your commitment and gives your subconscious mind
many hours to assimilate it. Often athletes go through the mo-
tions of the game, mentally, the night before. This gives the
mind time to absorb what the body will perform the next day.

Step Four: Have Courage

Success for one person may only be a brief stop for another.
Imagine a huge ladder. On the ground level, all the people are
dreaming of reaching the same goals. Some never step up to
the first rung. They dream, but don't move. Others are content
just to reach the second or third step, but never aspire to climb
higher. The further up the ladder you go, the easier it becomes
because the competition diminishes. Fewer people have the
courage or the belief in themselves to go all the way to the top.
Reinvent yourself as a leader. You don't have to lead the pack;
you can simply lead yourself.

Are you accepting my challenge to reach your full potential? Or will you ignore it and stay where you are? Difficult
situations will arise. What's important is your decision to keep
trying. Go for it. Make the brave choice. Move up the ladder.
Just because other people have stopped along the way doesn't
mean you have to. When I'm fearlessly pursuing my goals I
feel most alive. So will you.

Step Five: Leave Room for Destiny

Sometimes, no matter how hard we work to change or conquer a problem, the outcome is not what we hoped for. Our high school sweetheart dumped us, we didn't get into our first college choice, we didn't get hired for the job we wanted. Each choice, each event slightly changes the direction of our life. How many times, years later, have we looked back and thanked our lucky stars that these events happened just as they did? Otherwise, we'd never be where we are right now. Remember, there is always the chance that a higher force—whether fate or destiny or God—has stepped in to make alterations according to some plan you don't yet see. Remember this as events change and redirect your course. Sometimes, if it's not meant to be, it's not meant to be. Something else just as great or far better can take its place. As hard as it is to accept a difficult event, it may be the catalyst that thrusts you into a more fulfilling life.

Remember

- Go into love standing firmly on your own two feet, strong within yourself, having a happy life, friendships, and goals of your own.
- Take charge! Beat the odds—overcome the obstacles, excuses, and fears that stop you from reaching your goals.
- Tune out the negative voices, including the one in your own head. Just because others can't do it doesn't mean you can't.
- Set your expectations high. Think big!
- Working on your goal is worth the risk. Your life will become an enjoyable, challenging journey full of growth and forward momentum.
- Your goals should guide you not blind you. Enjoy the journey toward your goals as you cultivate your relationships with the people you love.
- The greatest gift you can give anyone is your own happiness.

- Surround yourself with successful people you admire, who will lend you support in pursuing your goals.
- If you can't fix a problem, accept your losses and move on.
- Your goals are worthwhile and you have what it takes to reach them. No man will be bored once you get a life.

2

....

Dare to Grow

....

For years, Katie had been investing sporadically. She lis-
tened to some of her friends and bought what the in-
vestment community recommended. One year it was the
cosmetic enhancement companies like "Wrinkles B Gone,"
the next it was the exercise equipment conglomerates such
as "Thighs R Us." But within months they all plummeted,
leaving Katie with little to show for her investment. One
day, she saw an investment opportunity she hadn't no-
ticed before. It was the Katie New Opportunities Fund. "In-
vest in myself! Now there's a brilliant idea," she thought.
Since then, Katie has been getting wealthier by the day,
with no end in sight.

We live in a material world driven by the marketplace. Even
love has become a marketable commodity. Fragrance and cosmetic companies, magazines, beer makers; everyone is selling
love and sex. It's hard to believe that what counts is on the inside when we're bombarded with the message that our thighs
are too fat, our breasts are too small, our faces too wrinkled,
our hair too thin. Inundated with so many images of perfec-
tion, it's not surprising that we feel inadequate and wonder
how on earth we'll ever measure up. Several years ago, a news
story revealed that computer photo imaging takes inches off of
famous models' thighs for magazines and catalogs. Our images of beauty are so distorted that our ideals are often based
on retouched photos.

Not only did Melanie feel her face and body weren't pretty

enough, she also felt very fragile inside. Memories, especially difficult events from her childhood, were buried, but not forgotten. At the time, these problems frightened, angered, or deeply saddened her. But she felt okay now, content that she'd made it through. Within the safe environment she had created for herself, she was fine. Her life seemed to run smoothly until she met Brian. He was handsome, successful, and so attentive. She wondered what he saw in her. She obsessed over her hair and clothing before every date. As she began to open herself up to love, reaching out for a mature relationship, forgotten feelings and fears surfaced. Still deeply affected by her past, she started to fall apart because she had never dealt with these issues. Unable to have a close, intimate relationship, she shut down, and the emotional upheaval began. Before finding a great guy she needed to know herself and rid her life of old hurts and needs.

In order to change her long-held behavioral patterns, Melanie had to dig deep. To fall in love in a healthy way, she needed first to love and understand herself. Then she could enter a relationship with confidence and trust rather than neediness and fear. By questioning what made her the way she was and then working on herself, she slowly developed confidence. Instead of dramatically changing her behavior, looks, or personality to conform to Brian's or anyone else's standards or expectations, she needed to find her true self for her own sake. We all have changes we can make to become the great person we can and should be.

Dare to grow. No amount of perfume, clothing, plastic surgery, or guidance on how to find and keep a man will do you any good, unless you're prepared to make yourself whole on the inside. The biggest gift you can give yourself is to invest in your own growth. If you are proud of who you are, what you stand for, your ability to love, and how much you contribute to the lives of those around you, it will be easy to love yourself and to gain the interest and admiration of others. Confidence is one of the most attractive qualities a woman can have, and it comes from really knowing and believing in yourself.

Sadly, like Melanie, many women lack self-confidence. They stay with a man for fear of being alone. Some believe they don't deserve a great guy. Others fear abandonment. To make matters worse, when you have no self-esteem or goals and are weak and vulnerable, you tend to attract men who want to change or control you. Once you are stronger and no longer looking for someone to "save" you, your needs will change. You'll find yourself looking for a completely different man.

These five simple steps will help you reach deep down and learn to understand and love yourself. They are followed by important tips on opening up to others. This is a difficult exercise. Your first thought may be "See ya I'm going anywhere to avoid this." But hang on, once you know yourself and begin giving to others, you'll automatically start to change and grow into your best self.

Five Basic Steps to Personal Growth

Step One: Question Everything

Even if you want to change, it's hard to know how. In order to grow, start to question everything, even the beliefs you thought were set in stone. What do you care about? Who are the people you love? Start with the basics. What do you do? What are your interests? Why are those your interests? What do you value? (If you don't know what your own values are, how can you possibly look for them in someone else?) How do you react to other people? Why do you react that way? If you sense you're always angry, try to discover why, and who you're really angry at. Is it old anger or new anger? By asking yourself these questions you can start to remove the layers of your own opinions and others' opinions and get back to the truth of your own intuition. Another idea is to delve into these issues on paper. Writing slows your mind down and can help you get in touch with your feelings. It's a safe place to purge and let it all out. So ask those challenging questions. For example, why did

Melanie care about what she looked like? Why did she care about how she dressed? What is this saying about her? What is this saying about the people she's with? How important is this to you? Is it more important than the things you do? Ask yourself, If everything were stripped away, all your beliefs and years of influence from others, what would be left? What is truly part of your soul, or reason for being? Don't walk blindly down the path of your life without considering the whys. Melanie realized that her friends loved her regardless of how her looks changed. She had created unrealistic expectations of what men found beautiful. Only after she realized this, could she see her own beauty.

Growing up we are deeply affected by how our parents treat us. We learn from them how to behave and how to love. Their perceptions of us and themselves all ultimately determine if we will feel dependent or independent, confident or insecure. Throughout our lives, people tell us who we are in relation to themselves, but in fact, we are more than what anyone sees. We are not only the child of our parents, the friend of our friends, the lover of our lovers. We are not *only* the reflection of others, rather, our real perception of self can only come from within, and this requires time and effort. After all, how we see ourselves has a lot to do with how others see us.

Shaw had been casually dating Carol for a month. One hot sunny Saturday they went with some friends for a boat ride to a private beach for the day. To his surprise, Carol had not brought a bathing suit. Attracted to her bubbly personality, Shaw would never had cared that Carol was slightly overweight. But her obvious embarrassment and insecurity made them both feel uncomfortable and prevented them from connecting. Carol's perception of herself turned Shaw's focus on imperfections he had never even noticed.

How we perceive ourselves also greatly influences our choices in men. It determines the kind of men we attract. An insecure woman will often attract a man who needs to be in control. If you haven't assessed yourself, you're likely to draw the wrong men and suffer through unsatisfactory relationships.

Step Two: Acknowledge Your Flaws

"The real fault is to have faults and not try to mend them."
— Confucius

The second step toward personal growth is acknowledging that there is room to change and develop. Accept that you are not perfect. Are you stubborn? Do you have a quick temper? Are you needy, clingy, lazy, bossy, irresponsible, selfish, judgmental or snobby? You have flaws, admit it! This doesn't mean you're a bad person; it just means that there are things in your character or personality that can be improved.

People are afraid to look at themselves; change scares them. It's only natural to be comfortable with our old familiar patterns, despite the fact they may be harming us. You may be thinking, "I don't want to change, and if you don't like it, Tough!" Yes, you can make excuses and fool yourself that your bad behavior is okay. You may even think that people should love you for your "real" self, warts and all. The reality is, you're doing yourself a great disservice. This attitude will stunt your growth and make a serious relationship almost impossible. These nonproductive patterns will overwhelm and distract others from focusing on your loving core. Redefining some rough edges may be all that lies between you and "the one."

Step Three: Get Specific About What You Need to Work on

The more you open up and expand your frame of reference, the faster you will grow. This means stepping out of the world you live in. Discover what you need to work on.

Look Realistically at Yourself How do you perceive yourself? Make a list of the things you like and those you don't. Don't forget to include traits others see in you, even if you can't see them in yourself. It might shock you to learn someone thinks you are selfish or controlling but it's important to examine why they think so. Then, in a second column, write down the qualities to which you aspire. It's time to phase out any negative traits that hinder your growth and embrace the positive qualities on your list. For example, for those who are always acquiescing to others' needs while burying their own, acknowledging and delivering on your own needs would be listed in your "aspirations column."

Being able to adapt, change, and grow is crucial to our personal development. Melanie's attitude was: "I'm sick of things the way they are, and I'm willing to try something new to improve them." It took courage for her to face reality and examine her imperfections. But it became one of those moments in her life that would define and shape her future. The catalyst that moves us toward growth is different for us all. A scary move to a job or city. Getting out of a bad relationship, even making a new friend outside your familiar circle are outward moves from security. Any of these events can inspire us to take a long, hard look at ourselves. It's often the more subtle choices, like, acts of kindness, a few extra hours on a project, taking time to meditate, working out, or stopping negative behavior that shape our destiny.

Ask for Feedback   We tend to shut out and fight the people who threaten our identity. We build up enormous psychological barriers to people who push our buttons, revealing in us truths we don't want to see. In defending our egos these barriers often filter out reality and hold us back from growing. Challenging or changing our identity by adding unfamiliar ideas can evoke fear. It's frightening not to know what lies ahead. Most people see criticism as proof that they're a failure or are not loved enough, something they would rather not admit. In reality, you only hold yourself back if you do not recognize and acknowledge your weaknesses.

Self-awareness helps you grow and develop confidence. Knowing how others see us can be a powerful force in our growth and can enhance our relationships. Friends or lovers can help you find out what's inside of you if you're ready to see it by illuminating blind spots. You already know the people who are going to tell you the truth, so ask a few of them to write down five qualities they consider your greatest attributes and five qualities they feel are your greatest weaknesses. This will be hard, as many friends will feel if they're truly honest you won't forgive them. Assure those who are reluctant that you're just doing homework and won't be upset by their comments. If they sugarcoat everything to protect your feelings, you'll learn nothing. You might be surprised at how happy they are to find you finally willing to listen to their gripes. It will be good practice for you to listen without answering back or debating with them. When you get the lists and compare them to one another, you'll probably find they match up on more than a few counts. Remember, you can't grow until you know, so remain open to these perceptions. Your first challenge may be to thank them.

Once you have the lists, don't be sad, discouraged, or angry about the feedback you've received. It was given to you by people who love you, and now you can start to blossom. If they suggest you are spoiled, arrogant, or even too nice, and you don't understand how they could see you this way, be as open as possible to their perceptions of your behavior. Bite your tongue when you're tempted to argue or become defensive. Focus on your own revelations, hear the message rather than getting stuck in feeling ashamed, attacked, or blamed. Listen objectively. Remember: You're here to learn and their input is helpful. Only by knowing your weaknesses can you develop and improve. Have you ever had the experience of a close friend telling you something about yourself—"You don't like to share" or "You're very judgmental"—in a very offhanded way? Often we are surprised since it seems so alien to how we view ourselves. Listen to those hints! They are guiding you gently. If you don't like it, examine yourself honestly and work on changing this behavior.

Just because the people in your life aren't telling you anything doesn't mean they aren't bothered by some of your behavior. Many of your actions that bother your friends also may turn off the men in your life. So many times I have heard women say, "I wish he would tell me why he left" or "I wish I knew earlier those little things that bothered him. I would have been willing to examine those things in our relationship." Most men don't give us the opportunity to hear their list of complaints. They just move on. Brad, a handsome Southern catch, had this to say: "I don't want to start an argument, fight, or hurt her feelings over something hard to change. I'd rather date someone without those characteristics."

As much as we might not like negative feedback from our friends, their loving concern is really a gift not a judgment. It's helpful to consider different perspectives on how others perceive you now, rather than getting hurt by a love interest later. Once you understand how you come across you can decide on what changes you wish to make and start working and growing. If you trust that your friends and family truly want to help you, this exercise will be very helpful. In my experience it has never backfired when people find the courage to get on a personal growth track. Without a doubt, it leads to greater fulfillment and joy.

Step Four: Commit to Growth

> "Come to the edge," he said. They said, "We are afraid." "Come to the edge," he said. They came. He pushed them . . . and they flew.
>
> —Guillaume Apollinaire

Now that you have made your own list and received feedback from others, it's time to make the commitment and do the work.

There is a lot of power in saying things out loud. Tell a few of your supportive friends and family members what you have learned and have decided to focus on. Repeat it to yourself out loud, write it down, and leave it on your bedside table; for example, "I am going to control my temper. When I feel my temperature rising, I'll take a deep breath and remind myself it doesn't serve me to lose control. I'll choose a more appropriate way to express my feelings." Go for a run, take a long shower, go to a funny movie, dance to your favorite music, go to a reflective spot you love. Be proud of yourself for following through! Every time it will get a little easier. Here's another example: "I will speak up. I will make myself heard." A friend, Anne, was shocked when her best friend had the nerve to suggest that she was emotionally closed. Once she heard it, Anne recognized it was true and set about changing herself. "At first it took a lot of effort; I traced it back to not feeling safe. I have to remind myself at emotional moments that this person cares; it's safe to share what I'm feeling," Anne says. "But like straightening my posture, after a little while, it started to feel natural."

Step Five: What You Focus on = Reality

"Imagination is more important than knowledge."
—Albert Einstein

Whatever you focus on grows. Take advantage of this phenomenon! Become aware of the way it operates in your life. If you focus on your friendships, they will flourish. If you focus on bringing love into your life, you will bring love into your life. Be warned that negative thoughts also beget negative results—if you focus on your fear, for instance, it intensifies. Your mind can actually accelerate movement and momentum toward a new reality. Imagine the optimal you, the optimal man, the optimal life. Take your wish list and pin it up near your bed. As you drift off to sleep, hold this image of the new you. In your mind, you are already this person. Envision yourself in your future and imagine the way it feels. This will help you be much more comfortable and less afraid of achieving it. The steps needed to get there will also become clearer. The more you practice this, the stronger your vision will become.

Opening Your Heart to Others

"Often we underestimate the power of a touch, a smile, a kind word, a listening ear, honest compliment, or the smallest act of caring—all of which have the potential to turn a life around."

—Leo Buscaglia

The greatest reward in life is to feel that you have made a positive difference in others' lives. Yet it is surprising how often people pass up the opportunity to help others, even their own friends and family. Closed and protective, many people think that by giving to someone else there will be less for them. In fact, just the reverse is true. By going just slightly out of your way, you can potentially make a big difference in someone's life, while enriching your own. One of my friends was hospitalized for a few weeks. On one of my visits I met another friend of hers, Leslie, who had driven 160 miles to be there. I was moved by her devotion and we immediately became friends. The spirit of love and caring developed when two strangers, visiting a mutual friend in the hospital, met and became lifelong friends.

Make a commitment to yourself to do one thing a day to make a difference, even if it's small. Be there for a friend, help someone on the street, donate time to a good cause, stay late to help clean up after a party, hold open a door, ask someone sitting alone at lunch to join you, give up your seat on the bus or subway, make a phone call to help someone get a job, apartment, or date. If you can help someone, do it! The long-term rewards of being open and extending yourself to others are great. The more you help people, the easier and more natural it will become, and you'll feel great.

Today, make a commitment to yourself that you're not going to be judgmental or negative. Here are some ways you can start making a difference:

Start with Those Close to You

Most people know who they can count on in an emergency. It's natural, when you're in need, to call those who have the capacity to give and listen. Start *being* one of these people by reaching out to friends and family.

Making money and achieving success or celebrity in our careers—none of these things reward or fulfill us as much as making a positive difference in someone else's life. The first step toward giving more is to pay attention: watch, listen, and be aware of what you can do to help those around you. Look around and do what you can do to make life easier for someone you love.

If you don't know where to start, try giving and sharing something you enjoy. My friend Runa loves to cook. It's hard work, and typically she's running around while others are enjoying her wonderful creations. Her pleasure comes from knowing that people really appreciate the great food she makes. Is it any surprise that people are drawn to her giving nature?

Strangers Are People, Too

At a friend's wedding where I knew only a few acquaintances, I was struck by how unfriendly everyone was. The guests didn't know one another; the bride and groom were too busy to make introductions. Strangers just weren't interacting. Then Elissa entered the room. I watched her; she had a warm smile and greeting for everyone. I wondered who she was and how she knew so many people. Later that evening I had the chance to ask her. "I met the bride backpacking in Europe. I just flew in from Brazil yesterday and I hadn't met anyone before today." Nobody, thankfully, had told Elissa that it wasn't the social norm here to be so open, friendly, and attentive.

We've been taught since childhood that strangers are a threat, and we withhold our trust. We can justify not loving or caring for people when we label them as "different." While there is a place for caution, we need to use what we've learned to break down the barriers. By hanging on to this conditioning, we are missing all sorts of opportunities to make new friends. Who is this stranger? More often than not, he or she is someone who yearns for love, longs for acceptance, and wonders if they're good enough. They share many of the same fears and dreams as you do.

I know strangers can be a threat and we all feel safest in our inner circle. But because of my unusual circumstances I had a different perspective. I learned early in life that not all strangers are to be feared; they can be a great gift. I suffered years of abuse as a young child, at the hands of my stepmother. To me, a stranger was not a threat, but a symbol of freedom from the pain I was enduring at home. Strangers, people whom I was not expected to trust (as I was expected to trust my stepmother), proved kinder, more reliable, and more loving than those closest to me. If I did well at a school sports event there was always a teacher or older student to acknowledge me with a pat on the back or with encouragement. Stewardesses, shopkeepers, bus drivers, neighbors . . . wherever I went someone would ask me about my interests, offer a compliment, or make me feel special. Such human kindness offered a welcome relief and helped me through a nightmarish time in my life. Without the help and support from some of those "strangers," I would not have grown to be the woman I am today.

I am not suggesting you should indiscriminately welcome every stranger into your heart. Of course, there are people that you should be watchful of and might not want to know, so use your common sense. Rather, acknowledge that some of the strangers around you could be wonderful, special, big-hearted people who are waiting to be transformed into friends. If you believe that things happen for a reason, then know that this stranger in need has crossed your path at this particular time and place so that you could make a difference in his or her life.

Most people don't even break out of their little social clique to experience the world. Open your eyes and heart to exploring the many new experiences and people life offers outside your universe. Meeting new people and expanding your social group is often the key to meeting Mr. Right.

One of my best friends, Sue, a Canadian who was in New York getting her degree, noticed a good-looking guy waiting at the crosswalk. She realized he was the same guy she had seen near her school, so she turned to him and broke the ice with, "Didn't I see you at NYU?" They walked the next five blocks together and dated for the next two years. The moral of the story? Being afraid to open the door to a stranger is not the answer. Learning to become a good "people reader" is. Keep your eyes and ears wide open; become part of humanity, not a fearful child. If Sue had not taken the risk and started a conversation, she would never have met this wonderful man. He would have become one of the hundreds of people she passed by on the street. Being responsive and open to strangers becomes easier each time. You'll be surprised how people will respond in kind.

Don't Hurt Others—and Stand up to the People Who Do!

How often has someone said something mean-spirited that hurt your feelings? Feels awful, doesn't it? Have there been times when you've been critical or talked about someone behind their back? Too often we don't give enough thought to the far-reaching consequences of our words or actions. Some people even revel in hurting others. Take Nancy, for example. On the New York City social scene, Nancy is famous for spreading the most mean-spirited and up-to-date gossip. She forms her exaggerated, hurtful opinions by combining fragments of gossip she hears and then reintroduces these opinions as facts. Through the years, I have seen many a good person's reputation marred by Nancy and others like her. Remember, there is a big difference between a fact and a rumor. The sad thing is, although no one likes Nancy, everyone is polite to her. They're afraid of becoming her next victim. If you maliciously spread nasty rumors that could hurt someone's life, then you're a gossip. Even if you only pass along this gossip, you're just as responsible as those who created the information. Get a life of your own and you'll be so busy working, creating, and building that you won't have time to tear down other people's lives. If you want to make a difference, stand up to the Nancys of the world and tell them you don't want to participate in their negative comments. There is an old saying: "Evil will flourish if good men do nothing."

Nice girls sometimes put up with nasty, catty girls because they want to be part of the "in crowd." They want to belong and feel accepted. Don't buy into anyone's twisted, negative value system or lifestyle, even if they are perceived as "cool." These attitudes can be contagious. If you want to move forward and make changes in your life, you must keep out negative influences and bring in the positive people who will be there to help you move forward.

Soon after I moved to New York, I overheard a woman say, referring to me, "She's being so nice to me; what does she want?" It's a sad thing when friendliness is interpreted as opportunism. Catch yourself and your perceptions when a newcomer is friendly or reaches out. Everyone's life is already full of challenges, hurdles, and bumps in the road. Make an effort to help them move forward with their lives; don't hurt or cause them pain.

Remain Open

It takes patience and practice to open up to the people around you. It's not easy to take off the armadillo armor that you may have built up, layer upon layer, over the years. Although it may make you feel safe, this armor isolates the love and warmth of the people near you; it stops them from seeing that there is a real person hiding underneath.

It's natural to build a barrier around your heart after you've been hurt, disappointed, or manipulated. Pretty soon, however, you may be walled in. Every person you meet afterward faces the challenge of permeating those walls. If they do break through and you're again disappointed, you tend to make it even harder for the next.

It's important to protect yourself, but being overcautious can also alienate exactly the kind of man you want—one ready for a committed relationship. Will he have the patience to break through so he can get to know you?

Look Behind the Toys and Flash

In Jim's eyes, the ideal woman is tall, has a thin body, great legs, and large breasts. For Paula, the perfect man is well built, tall, dark, handsome, rich, and drives a sports car. For Jim and Paula it's not about love; it's about playing with toys. They depend on these labels to tell them who they are. Jim thinks of himself as "the successful investment banker" and Paula as "the girl with a great figure." They've forgotten about being human, and are identifying with an object or role. Paula feels good today because she looks good. If she doesn't look good tomorrow, she won't feel good. If Jim loses his cool job, he'll lose his identity.

Paula is not what she wears, and Jim is not what kind of car he drives. Their qualities and character are what's important. What makes them who they are is what they do and how they feel when no one's looking. Does Paula have a warm heart, compassion, empathy, and intelligence? Does Jim? Toys are fun, but they can't nourish anyone on the inside.

People often talk about "inner beauty." It's almost a *Vogue* cliché. But think about those people you most admire. What makes them special? Is it how they look and what they own, or is it who they are on the inside? Is it the size of their wallets? Or is it what you see in their eyes and heart? The qualities you choose to wear inside are the ones that truly matter.

Good Manners

People running quickly on the treadmill of life make excuses that they are too busy to care, too busy to return a call, too busy to send a thank-you note when someone has clearly gone out of their way for them. What happened to plain old good manners? They are really pretty simple. Thank everyone who extends themselves to you.

Everyone, from the elevator man to the CEO, deserves to be treated courteously and with respect. Politeness is especially important in big cities, where so many people walk around feeling anonymous or self-important, making excuses to be rude, pushy, and totally unobservant. Having good manners starts with being thoughtful and caring. It helps to remember that the way you treat people in everyday situations makes a difference to each of their lives. And remember, you affect not only those around you, but those around them and so on.

Imagine it as a room full of helium balloons. If you hit one balloon, it sets all the others around it in motion, an effect that eventually moves out to almost every balloon in the room. We don't realize the extent of our power and how much good kind, thoughtful words or actions can do. Conversely, rude, thoughtless behavior can cause much more damage than we may imagine. If you see yourself as able to make a positive difference in people's lives, your interactions with strangers will become meaningful. If you enjoy them, you'll be able to initiate them with ease not fear. Of course, you can't please everyone, but it takes no extra time to be respectful, thoughtful, polite, and to use good manners!

Give to Givers

In an ideal world, we would all give for the joy of giving. In the real world, however, whatever givers have to give, takers will always be there to take. There comes a time when givers are giving everything away to takers and inevitably feel, "I'm always there for everyone else; why is nobody ever there for me?" Giving unselfishly means expecting nothing in return, but when we continue to give to takers, that's what we get back—nothing. So give to others who are also willing to give. Givers deserve to feel the rewards of being appreciated, loved, and having someone there for them. It's time to do your spring cleaning. Go through your address book and circle in red the people who give back, who would come visit you in the hospital or who you can count on in an emergency. Spend more of your time giving to the people who give to you.

A friend remarked, "I'm too nice. I get walked on by everybody." I replied, "No, you're not too nice. You're just too nice to the wrong people!" Often our friendships have developed by chance, at school, in the neighborhood, or at the office. Places or circumstances brought you together. You weren't choosing your friends based on who was the kindest person you met and who best reciprocated your friendship. How many of these chance friends are takers? Most takers are cynical, distrustful, and suspicious. As the saying goes, their glass is perpetually empty and in need of filling. And often the people who give the most are taken for granted and not appreciated. Yet these givers are the people we should all try to emulate. Appreciate them, celebrate them—hopefully, you will encourage and inspire yourself and others to be more like them.

Allow Others to Give to You

Kim, always thoughtful and generous, is afraid of other givers. She's happy to extend compliments, emotional support, energy, and gifts, but is uncomfortable receiving them. Afraid of the intimacy true love demands, Kim avoids it altogether by attaching herself to one taker after the next. This way, she always has an excuse for why she can't fall in love. But the truth is, she's not up to an equal partnership, a real connection. If you're already generous in heart and spirit, ask yourself if you're giving to takers to subconsciously keep yourself from a real connection.

When love flows back and forth equally, the emotional level that you can reach is much higher and the commitment deeper and stronger. By giving to givers, you're assured that your good will is reciprocated and won't go unappreciated. Givers will be there when you are in need. Once you bask in the glory

will be much easier to recognize another. Every-
nate and friends who give back.

Dare to Care

*"What do we live for if it is not to make life less difficult for
each other."*

—George Eliot

When I was in India many people scolded me for giving
money to starving children. "You are encouraging them to
beg," they said. "If you help one, ten more will be behind him,
so why even bother?" The excuses people make in order not to
feel guilty are incredible. It's frightening to know they let these
feeble, empty excuses protect them from feeling the need to act
and care. Wouldn't it be much better when you see someone in
need of help to make a difference instead of an excuse? You can
transform yourself into a giver, someone who not only responds to the needs of others, but is proactive and anticipates
where she can be of help. In times of crisis, all humans gravitate toward givers, the people who are willing to put on their
boots and help us wade through the swamp of life. When you
start caring and extending yourself to others in a proactive
way, you'll be amazed at the ways they will reciprocate and
support you. Both lives are enriched.

I believe that we can't love one person until we love people
in general. In other words, until we see strangers as real people, with feelings that can be hurt, we cannot truly recognize
and love anyone. Without empathy and kindness for our fel-
low human beings, we cannot be open to a healthy, happy
love with that one special man. The same place within us that
creates empathy and awareness for the needs of a complete
stranger also cares for those who are close to us.

You gain so much by opening your heart. Tell an elderly
woman how wonderful she looks. Hold someone's door open.
Compliment someone on their garden, child, hat. Buy some
food for a homeless person. Help anyone who crosses your

path that is obviously in need, even if it only means brightening their day with a smile or encouraging words.

Remember

- Acknowledge the way you are and decide what it is you would like to improve about yourself.
- Getting feedback is an available and underutilized source of information. Use it.
- Make a difference by caring, extending yourself, and loving.
- Work together. We are all traveling the same road.
- Look for the similarities in others not the differences.
- Reach out to humanity. You will feel the personal rewards immediately!

3

....

Nurture Your Friendships

....

Friendship is responsible for at least half of the happiness in the world.

—Aristotle

Katie and Anna were at the gym, the sound of their footsteps pounding on the treadmill, as they whiled away the time by watching bad daytime TV. Anna rolled her eyes at the talk show's subject, "My girlfriend was abducted by aliens."

"Speaking of abducted," said Katie, "whatever happened to Louise? She hasn't shown up for our workout in weeks."

"I know," replied Anna, her voice breathless as she ran. "She hasn't surfaced for air ever since she started dating that Dave guy. She totally disappears from life when she's in dating mode, no return phone calls, no time for friends."

"Wow, I can't imagine that," said Katie. "I mean, when I went out with John, my friends were my alternative source of advice, support, and sanity! I wouldn't give that up for anyone! Besides, if it wasn't for our regular wine-and-pasta-fest dinners, we wouldn't need to come here, and there's nothing like a workout with a good friend."

Both laughed, knowing how true it was.

Female friendship is a sacred sorority where we can share our innermost feelings and still feel safe. Let's face it: Significant others can understandably feel threatened by long talks of past lovers, current relationship problems, or future fantasies. There are some things you are only going to save for your best girlfriends. Don't overlook the importance of cultivating a strong group of relationships among women friends to support you. These close emotional and spiritual bonds can last us a lifetime. Girlfriends can also be key strategic allies in meeting the man of your dreams. While you're out having fun with them, you can also meet other interesting people.

Too many of us expect that the right man will make us happy in every way. But this expectation can lead to disappointment. The more friends you have, the more support and wealth you bring to your intimate relationships. Each adds value to our life in a different way.

There is a great saying, "Your friends will know you better in the first minute you meet them than your acquaintances will know you in a thousand years." We share our hearts and minds with friends. The bonds that link us are mutual respect, love, compassion, and support. Our good friends know, understand, and accept us as we are. Through them we learn about our shortcomings and so are able to grow within the warmth of their love.

Despite the incredible benefits of friendship, it's amazing how many people do not know how to be or keep a good friend. Remember, to get a life we all need friends. Practicing the following ten tips helped me develop and nurture an incredibly strong friendship network in a new city.

Make Time

Organize regular get-togethers. Spending quality time together nurtures the relationship and lets them know how much you care. Remember, love is as much of an action as it is a feeling. Make an effort to give time and energy to your friends, both male and female, and keep up on what's happening in their lives. This will ensure you keep a healthy perspective on your own life. We often think we need to see people one-on-one, but I've found gathering several of my friends together for monthly dinners can be an extremely effective way of keeping people together, sharing and cultivating a community.

Call and get all your good friends' email addresses. With the touch of a finger you can send out updates, invitations or a personal note. Write a letter to someone you've lost touch with. Tell her why you valued her friendship.

Stand by Your Word

If you say you'll do something or be somewhere, don't let your friend down. Your word is who you are. If someone can't depend on you, then you're not being a good friend. This goes for keeping secrets, too. If someone trusts you enough to tell you something private, don't betray that trust. Practicing keeping commitments on a daily basis on the small things will result in your own personal sense of integrity, which will resonate with everyone you come in contact with.

Work Together

I introduced my friends to each other. This helped to develop and nurture a group of special, supportive people to build my future with. I could express my deep desires and wishes to them. Confiding my dreams to them helped propel me toward reaching my goals. We encourage and support one another and commit ourselves to helping one another succeed. Ask yourself what you can do to make your friends' lives easier—then do it.

In addition to the fact that female friendships are valuable in their own right, they'll become particularly helpful when you start to go out together to meet new men. Once you've found a great guy, your friends can have a strong influence on him, too. As one man said to me about one of my girlfriends, "I was so impressed by how much everyone loved her. I felt lucky to be with someone so many people thought was wonderful."

You know your heartfelt words to others about a friend's positive qualities can help, so express them generously.

Don't Compete

Don't compete with your friends for men. I know a group of unmarried women in New York City who see every woman as a competitor. They are automatically catty and cruel, making up ridiculous stories about popular women (in some cases their own friends) in hopes of turning potential suitors off and lessening their own competition. Smart men see right through these women's fake smiles. Don't be one of the "shark" women. There are plenty of men out there. No man is worth sabotaging your friends.

A male friend of mine had a good example of team playing: "I met Ann, a spectacular girl, at the local pub after work. What I didn't know at the time was that she was in the middle of working things out with a guy she'd been seriously involved with for two years. The chemistry was there, but the timing was bad. She invited me to a party, and I talked to her interesting roommate Jane for two minutes. The next day, when I called to thank her, she disclosed her circumstances and asked if she could set me up with her roommate, who thought I was very nice. I ended up dating Jane for some time." Most girls in Ann's position would try to keep the new guy on the back burner, just in case. They wouldn't think about setting him up with a friend. Ann proved herself thoughtful and classy when, unable to date this man herself, she did something nice for her friend.

Don't Dump Your Friends for a Man

Friendships are valuable. Don't neglect your girlfriends just because you've met a new guy. When an exciting new man pulls your time and attention away from a best friend, it's easy for that friend to feel let down. Avoid this by letting your close friends know that you need a few months to get comfortable in your relationship, to spend a little extra time getting to know him. Sit them down and assure them how much their friendship means to you and that this stage is temporary. Tell them you don't want this new relationship to hurt your friendship, and ask them if they wouldn't mind being patient with you for just a few months. Address this issue head-on by letting them know how much you love them. Men may come and go, but your girlfriends should be there forever.

Introduce him to your friends. If he gets along with them it will only help to solidify the relationship. Don't stay glued to his side. Give him breathing space to make his own connection with the people you love. As we listen to our own inner guidance, we need to take into consideration what those who love us feel. If none of your friends approve, listen to what they have to say. How many times have we all said or heard, "You were completely right about that jerk"? Love is notoriously blind; friends can help open our eyes.

Remember Birthdays

Find out when all of your friends' birthdays are and create a birthday list by month in your permanent phone book. At the beginning of every year, enter them in your date calendar. It sounds like a small thing, but it's a great way to stay in touch and to let your friends know you're thinking about them. Instead of shopping impulsively, listen all year long for clues to what friends or loved ones might enjoy as a gift and pick it up months in advance.

Be Honest

When asked if a dress looks good, don't be afraid to be open and honest. (Tell them, "I love you, but I assume you want an honest answer. It really doesn't compliment your figure." Tell them before they leave the house—not at the party.) Your friends will learn to trust you and appreciate your candor if it's done sensitively. After all, if your friends aren't going to tell you the truth, who will? Give constructive criticism and encouragement about issues you feel can positively help their lives. Just make sure you do it with love. There's nothing wrong with being direct and honest, as long as you are ready to hear the reply, "You know what? I like myself that way." Be prepared to love your friends, flaws and all. Above all, be gentle and be ready for your friends to be honest with you, too. Being honest also means expressing your love. Tell them often how important they are, celebrate them.

Just Listen

Sarah was in trouble. She'd lost her job and her boyfriend in the same month. She started to withdraw from everyone. I let her know, in no uncertain terms, that I cared and would be right there beside her, no matter what happened. As I repeated this her loneliness and doubt was replaced with love and hope. Sarah told me that when she had tried to talk to several friends about what was hurting her they belittled her problems. "It just made me feel worse." What she really needed was to talk things through and have someone listen, empathize, and share their own experiences.

You never know when you'll be in Sarah's shoes, thankful for a friend's full presence, understanding, and love. Just being there for a friend in need will so strengthen a bond that it will often result in a friendship for life. There is nothing more comforting than a friend whom you know will guide you through the hard times and make the good times much richer.

Don't Take Sides

We were best friends traveling in Europe. Tired after a long, hot car ride, we finally reached our hotel. As I carried what I considered to be way too much of Adrienne's luggage from our small car, we launched into a heated argument. I turned to Leslie for validation. "I'm sick of lugging all her stuff around." Adrienne fired back, "Jenny packs hardly anything, borrows all my clothes, and then complains I bring too much!" When two good friends fight, each wants someone to be on their side—to validate their feelings. Taking sides does not help. Fueling the fire and saying "That jerk!" or yes-ing them will only make things worse. Instead, let them know you care about them and support them, then make a positive contribution by helping both to look at what they need to work on within themselves to solve the conflict. Although people appreciate honest assessments, they will appreciate them more readily if you're diplomatic. If both people put their guard up and think they're totally right, then nothing will get resolved. In the heat of the conflict, Leslie grabbed both of our hands, put them in the air, and started singing "That's What Friends Are For." This silly solution worked. She had reminded us that our commitment to the friendship was stronger than this disagreement.

Swallow Your Pride

Sometimes miscommunication, selfishness, immaturity, stubbornness, or even pettiness can break up a close friendship. It's always better to swallow your pride than to lose a relationship. Think about calling or writing that old friend or sibling you had a falling out with. Tell them that you realize you don't want to go another month or year without them in your life. Be honest about your feelings. As hard as that call is, the rewards of renewing that friendship are far more valuable than being right! If that person was capable of the kind of communication, support, and love you seek in your life, don't let them go. It's much easier to maintain a friendship than to regain it.

Now that you are becoming happier with your own life, we can move on to Part II, finding the right man.

Remember

- Friends are the cornerstones of our lives. Treat them well.
- Spend time focusing on helping your friends reach their goals.
- Help your friends shine by always presenting them in the best possible light.
- It's simple: If you want to have a friend—be a friend.

PART II

....

Then
Get a Man

4

• • • • • • • • • • • • • • • • • • •

Master the Art
of Reading People

• • • • • • • • • • • • • • • • • • •

While window-shopping, Katie stopped to admire a display
of neon T-shirts.

"Oh please, Katie!" Anna winced as she pulled her away.
"Sometimes your choice in T-shirts is as dismal as your
choice in men."

"Look who's talking." Katie laughed. "Words of wisdom
from the girl who fell for Drippy Dan, Iceberg Ian, and
Limpy Leo!"

Arm in arm, they continued their search for the perfect
outfit.

Don't berate yourself over bad choices you've made in the past. We've all done it. Being an effective "people reader" will ensure that the choices you make in the future will be much better. In order to read people well, you've got to use your powers of observation everywhere you go. The more you're able to see and understand, the more confident and comfortable you'll be with new people and situations.

If you want to improve your chances of choosing a great man, you need to master the art of reading people. The first step is to be more observant. Here's an example: I was walking down Fifth Avenue. Ahead of me I noticed an elderly blind man and ahead of him a big sign on the curb saying DANGER, FIVE-FOOT HOLE. It was lunch hour, and none of the workmen were there. There was no hard barrier up, just a huge neon sign and a four-inch plastic neon tape protecting the area. The blind man was walking directly toward the hole. There were about fifty well-dressed businesspeople walking by him and many more coming from the other direction. The blind man was walking slowly, so I slowed my pace and watched. Didn't anybody see that this blind man was walking right toward the manhole? Before danger could strike I grabbed his coat and steered him out of the way. Are people really so self-absorbed? Too focused on their own thoughts to see what's right in front of them? Are they too busy to care about a blind man on the brink of injury? I was shocked. Many people are completely unaware of what's going on around them. These same people don't stop to look around for the right partner, friends, or job. Instead, they settle for the status quo and join the army of "the walking blind." They are alive but not living consciously. This book is about regaining your power and finding and claiming for yourself a life that's going to make you happy—a life in which you *are* aware of the outside world. The first step to widening your receptivity is to stop focusing inward and look around you. Study the people you come in contact with. Until you learn to see everyone, you won't be able to see who's right in front of you.

Being a Voyeur

The way a person dresses can often provide clues about who he or she is. But as the saying goes, looks can be deceiving. It's much more important to find out who they are on the inside. Pay attention to a person's expressions and how they relate to others. Are they kind or rude? Serious or lighthearted? Body language is important. Do they carry themselves with confidence, or are they trying to hide? Are they physically cold and unaffectionate, or do they hug their friends when they meet? How do they relate to you? Do they take your hand and look you in the eye? Are they empathetic, making an effort to help others feel comfortable? Are they shy, sensitive, aggressive, territorial, strong, artistic, opinionated, practical, ambitious, emotional, soft-spoken? Pay attention. Ask friends or family members who you think read people well what they notice and look for.

As you turn your observations to men you are acquainted with, ask yourself: Is he aware of and sensitive to a woman's needs? Does he get along with and love his mother and sisters? All the information you gather will help you to read him better.

If you can learn to read people effectively, it will help you enormously, not only on the dating field, but in every area of your life. You'll be more aware of people's feelings and personality traits, and more aware of how others see you. Here are some more ways to become a good "people reader."

Watch People

The more you work at strengthening your powers of observation, the better you'll be at accurately reading strangers. Get used to the idea of studying people. If you're on the bus, at a party, or out shopping, take the time to watch the people around you. Try opening up all your senses rather than using your mind. Focus all your senses on them. Sight: What does their body language say? How do they move? With confidence, aggression, shyness? Are their shoulders rigid and tense? Do you see signs of their heart? Sound: What does their tone of voice tell you? How do you respond to it? Touch: Are they gentle, rough, affectionate? Do they radiate warmth and love? By studying strangers, you can train yourself to see the "big picture" and be well on your way to noticing all kinds of things you never thought you'd be able to see from just one look. There is so much information we miss. It's all there, you just haven't trained yourself to see it. Once you do, it will open up a whole new world. Push your awareness to a new level.

The Eyes Are the Window to the Soul

It's possible to read a lot about someone by studying their eyes. You just need to learn how and what to look for, and then you need to practice. Don't shy away from eye contact. Learning how to read eyes will change the way you see life.

The next time you look into a person's eyes, ask yourself these questions: Do they seem open and inviting or introverted and wary? Are they able to genuinely connect? Are they comfortable or uncomfortable? Are they analyzing you, too? Can you read their emotions? Do you see pain, joy, fear, compassion, strength, confidence, vulnerability? Eventually you'll be able to break through and see personality traits just by looking at someone's eyes. You may see that a person is holding back, critical and cautious, or is open and wanting to trust and connect.

Keep in mind the darker the eyes, the harder they are to read. It's also a lot easier to read someone when their eyes are facing the light. Like learning any language, the more you practice the better you become. With patience you will discover a wealth of information beneath the surface. One useful tip—our pupils get larger when we like what we're seeing.

Reserve Judgment

Your life experiences can help you assess others. On the other hand, prior experience can also blind you. If you only see others through the filter of your rose-colored glasses, you'll end up categorizing or labeling them. "This person must be like [this], because that's the experience I've had." Obviously, not everyone you meet will be kind or good. You have the right to screen people. But you don't want to make hasty, ill-founded assumptions. It's important to be aware of your inherent prejudices. The more you can put aside your preconceptions and accept others, the clearer your ability to read people will be. Karen, a twenty-three-year-old advertising executive, found Rich, the first lawyer she ever dated, controlling and argumentative. She vowed never to date another lawyer. Her friend wanted to introduce her to another guy who happened to work at the same firm. All her warning bells went off. Although Karen had never met him, she was already judging him.

You'll find that even the slightest prejudice can manifest itself and prevent you from having a meaningful relationship, so try to remain aware of any tendency you have to prejudge others. Each new person deserves a fresh chance. This means consciously asking yourself if you are being fair. Like Karen, many people just muddle through life without ever challenging or changing their beliefs and, as a result, they never grow. Reserve judgment and grow.

Empathize

Try to see the person behind the stranger. Look for commonalities not differences. Empathy is imagining yourself in someone else's shoes and allowing yourself to feel what they are feeling. When you meet new people, remind yourself that, like you, they are products of their environment. Try to see with your heart and hear with your eyes. You don't know what makes them the way they are. You don't know if they've had a bad day, were fired last week, or had an unhappy childhood. You don't know whether their life right now is a living hell for whatever reason. Perhaps they're doing the best they can, given their circumstances. It's not your place to judge people who seem unhappy or angry. Of course, you can always choose not to spend time with them. Some people change for the better, learning and becoming more empathetic. Others regress, closing themselves off and becoming bitter. Either way, remember some action or choice created their reaction. And some choice within you created yours.

Look for Personality Clues

Here are some very basic character types. Of course no one is going to fit perfectly into just one of these categories, but these may help you recognize certain traits and/or tendencies in men and in yourself. They may also help develop insights into the underlying currents that manifest in attraction, i.e., why certain types fit like a glove with other types.

Mr. Instant Coffee   Many brands to choose from. He's looking for instant gratification, and doesn't take long to percolate. Indiscriminately in pursuit of the "quick fix," he can be skillfully charming and spontaneous. Exciting, impulsive, irresponsible, and even immoral, his steeping hot come-on quickly becomes iced. Highly volatile when confronted, he rationalizes his behavior by blaming others. One taste and you know it's not the real thing. If he turns out to be a drip, freeze-dry him!

Renaissance Man   He's self-assured, focused, disciplined, and responsible, yet knows how to let loose and have fun. His intellectual and career interests are balanced with cultural and physical activities. Comfortable in jeans or a tux, this action man throws himself into his pursuits and is willing to fail. In touch with and expressive of his emotions, he exudes compassion and warmth as he crosses social and ethnic boundaries. Gathering eclectic and diverse admirers, the Renaissance Man knows what qualities he's looking for in a woman and is unlikely to be swayed.

The Fisherman   With patience he delivers the latest lines, lures, and tackles. Never happy or thankful with what he's got, he's constantly seeking a bigger catch. For the fisherman it's all about short term sport. Once you take the bait, you've lost the date. And once caught, you become the proverbial fisherman's tale—bigger than reality, or the one that got away. Either way, chances are you won't be a keeper.

Mr. Crusader   He's nurturing, empathetic and bighearted. Making a difference is more important than making money. Passionate in conversation, in his actions, and in bed. Fearless in his pursuit to save the world and solve everyone's problems except his own. Can give but has a hard time accepting criticism. Needs to be needed and is always there for his friends. After he fights Goliath he may not have much energy left— unless of course you're one of his projects. Be prepared to share him with the rest of the world.

The Chameleon   His personality is constantly changing to adapt to new situations. He blends into the crowd and shies away from the limelight. He attaches a high level of importance to being accepted; he is eager to please and tends to avoid conflict. Open-minded, flexible, accommodating, and likable, the chameleon will rarely say no or communicate any negative feelings. The chameleon lives for the moment, without large aspirations for the future.

The Boy Scout   Always solving everyone else's problems, scouts do more than their share. Charming, empathetic, loyal, dependable, protective, thoughtful, optimistic, practical, and unlikely to take sides in a conflict, he gives much more than he gets. It makes him feel good to make a difference. He obeys society's rules and saves his money wisely. A scout has an innate feeling of responsibility to help others and feels guilty when he takes—thus, his own needs often go unrecognized.

Bond, James Bond   This man likes his martini and his life shaken—not stirred. Not easily led, he makes his own path. He's powerful, secretive, strong, confident, bold, opinionated, adventurous, rebellious, expressive, and proud of his individuality. Undercover (or under the covers) he's seductive, mysterious, assertive, and irresistible. He's not afraid to speak his mind and enjoys playing devil's advocate. He's got all the latest gadgets and works best alone. Governed by a strong code of ethics, he'll quickly and wisely assess all the facts and swiftly execute his decision. Add olives; only serves one.

The "Whine" Steward   Focused on accumulating and obsessing over his own misfortunes, the "whine" steward will never turn down a good whine. He's grumpy, opinionated, close-minded, bored, unhappy, self-absorbed, and always complaining. He tends to be judgmental and critical. He will undermine the dreams and accomplishments of others. Usually fussy and never satisfied; he's angry at the world and pulls everyone down with him. Always expecting failure, he won't contribute to anyone's goals, including his own. Jealous of others' successes, the "whine" steward discourages hope and gloats over others' misfortunes. Needs a few more years to mature.

Mr. Wonderbread   Solid, basic, dependable, sensible, practical, mainstream, he has good values and a stable family. He's Mr. Nice Guy, a good friend. His life revolves around habits and rituals. He works nine to six, and is not very experimental or overly ambitious. He doesn't want to rock the boat, and he's not comfortable with extremes. Try adding some hot sauce to spice things up.

The Klingon   This man learned at a young age that by being and staying a victim he could find others to be financially and emotionally responsible for him—it worked well to remain helpless, dependent and clingy with few goals of his own. Uncomfortable being alone he seeks constant attention and is never satisfied. Selfish and self-centered, he believes society owes him. Unconcerned with the burdens he places on others, the Klingon looks for the easy way out by finding someone to take care of him. He needs to realize there's life on other planets.

The Ferrari   Quick, flashy, ambitious, and successful, there's no stopping the Ferrari as he speeds aggressively toward his destination. Because he moves at high velocity, his view of the world is distorted. Oblivious of his immediate environment, the Ferrari rarely stands still long enough to recognize how he affects those around him. He's a high-energy, high-maintenance gas guzzler. His ego is almost as big as his airbags. King of the road, his friendships and personal life often take a backseat (My way or the highway!). Put the brakes on and get him out of the car.

The Energizer Bunny Methodically marching forth fearlessly toward his goals, the Energizer Bunny finds bountiful energy to succeed in every area of life, both personally and professionally. Always on battery overdrive, it's hard for him to slow down and enjoy success. Often the offspring of critical parents, this power-driven bunny never feels he's accomplished enough. Thriving on stress and attaining many goals, his accomplishments are often more important than internal tranquillity. He keeps going and going and going . . .

The Rooster Cocky in appearance, flexing, constantly crowing about his sexual conquests—real or imagined—the rooster still lives in his high school or college football days; he may never have made the team, but he swaggers around pretending he did. He likes to pick fights in bars and always has to be in control. Overly self-assertive, he buys into traditional male/female roles and believes that this is a power struggle he must win. He believes himself to be a ladies' man but is really a chicken when it comes to getting in touch with his emotions. He may have grown up in a male-dominated family without enough influence from the henhouse.

The Bellhop The wary and cautious bellhop carries a lot of baggage. Not a good judge of character, he may have been hurt or taken advantage of by others and reacts to newcomers with anger and suspicion. Withdrawing to protect himself, he puts up boundaries and limits his exposure to new people. He's tired and hurt, cynical and withdrawn. His great desire and capacity to love is imprisoned by his fears, leaving him vulnerable, needy, and over-sensitive. He's slow to trust and make close friends and is quick to bail out of love relationships rather than be hurt again.

The Free Spirit   Drifting, flexible, uninhibited, and happy, the free spirit does not adhere to society's opinions or measures of success. Following his heart and inner voice rather than his ego, he is led to a career and hobbies that are aligned with his spirit and fulfillment. Strongly centered, he relishes life and his relationships. He's open-minded, accepting, and loving of others. He's happy alone or in a crowd. Committed to family, friends, and loved ones, free spirits want everyone to communicate with love. They embrace all that life has to offer.

Top Gun   Strong, outspoken, opinionated, intense, and impulsive, the top gun has a superiority complex. He feeds on autonomous control (no room for a copilot) and will do just about anything to get the upper hand and keep it, although his tactics may be well disguised. This high flyer needs an altitude adjustment. Exciting and powerful, he can be incredibly attractive for a while, but put your tray tables up, you may be in for some turbulence.

The French Poodle   His identity revolves around his pedigree. Nice to those in his circle but indifferent to everyone else. He's stubbornly self-righteous, inflexible, aloof, and unlikely to see another's point of view. The French poodle usually lives in a very small and narrow world by cutting off large portions of society. Holding himself above others so he'll feel better about himself, this man has an unmistakable sense of entitlement. Snobby, primped, fussy, and deeply insecure, he identifies himself through the groups he dislikes. Keep him on a short leash and have your pooper scooper ready.

The Chess Player   Always scheming and planning, the chess player will achieve his goals at any cost. He's afraid he'll never have enough or that what he has will be taken away; he would steal someone else's Queen and racks up many rooks in his path. He is manipulative, aggressive, inflexible, suspicious, and distrusting of others' moves. Check, no mate.

Mr. Hollywood   This attention hog always has some kind of Oscar-winning performance with which to entertain, but is quickly bored when the focus is not on him. Exciting and magnetic, he's full of energy. Mr. Hollywood is known for his generosity and mood swings. Motivated by a deep longing to be loved and accepted, he'll go to extraordinary lengths to feel fulfilled and at the center of attention. A shrewd manipulator, this womanizer talks prematurely of love to gain approval/acceptance. At times he can be emotionally childish, deliberately controversial and obnoxious.

I encourage you to notice other personality types based on your own experiences. Take an inventory of the guys you have known. See if you can figure out which types or combinations you have been attracted to and why. What values were important to you? What drew you in on a deep level? What repelled you or did not sit well with you? If you take the time to review your past attractions, your insight will improve immensely.

Remember

- Take the time to look, listen, and learn.
- When you look people in the eye, probe for personality clues.
- Preconceptions impair your ability to read others clearly.
- When you empathize and see another point of view, you gain greater insight.

5

Screening

Katie raced into the parking lot, screeching into the closest spot. Her stomach growled its approval as she grabbed hold of the shopping cart. She was starving! There was no stopping her; bagels, fruit, cheese, cookies, potato chips, everything—it all looked so good! Before you could say "Chocolate-covered almonds are healthy," the bags were in the trunk, and Katie was on her way home. As she put it all away, she suddenly stopped. "All this stuff and I have nothing for dinner!" Poor Katie had once again fallen into the "Shopping While Starving" syndrome. No shopping list, no plan . . .

Many single women feel they're on a quest for the ideal mate, that special someone who is an emotional and intellectual equal. They want someone interesting, kind, and loving who can fit into their circle of friends and who doesn't have a neurotic family. It's not always immediately apparent whether a new man fits your criteria. However, it is obvious that some don't. Can you really afford to invest one or two years in a relationship with a man, only to realize he doesn't have the long-term qualities you need, that his plans for the future don't coincide with yours? Of course not! So find out early by paying attention to your needs, experiences, and responses. If you're clear in advance about the qualities you require, you won't wait around to check out a man's romantic intentions. I'm not saying he'll be an "instant read." This process takes time; be patient and follow your instincts. By assessing whether a new man has the qualities you need, you'll be able to determine how well he fits your parameters. Simply put, this is "screening."

At twenty-seven, Lisa felt like she was going around in circles, falling in love with the wrong men over and over again. She wanted to stop the cycle but she didn't know how. She never actually analyzed why these relationships failed. Lisa didn't know exactly what she was searching for and got distracted by the wrong man. I suggested she pinpoint what it is she wants and then look for a man with those qualities. She needed to stop entering relationships blindly and stop committing herself to men who weren't compatible. "My old patterns were hard to break," Lisa acknowledged. "But it became so much easier once I realized why I was falling in love in the first place. I found out it hadn't been about love at all, rather about finding someone to take care of me."

You're about to embark on a dating adventure. For this you'll need certain tools to help you assess and screen the guys you'll be meeting. With your list defined you're not likely to be swept off your feet by peer pressure, a heavy come-on, his résumé, or chemistry alone. The more interactions and experiences you have, the clearer you will be on what you value. Think of it as an insurance policy, by effectively screening you minimize your downside.

Know What You Want

How can Lisa go forward and not make the same mistakes she'd made in the past? By going into her next relationship with open eyes and taking control of her life and making better choices. This means clearly identifying in advance what she's looking for in a man so she can find what *she* wants.

If you are newly single, the dating scene can be particularly overwhelming. Remember Katie's shopping trip? If you're really famished when you go to the supermarket, you end up buying junk food that won't satisfy, certainly isn't good for you, and will probably go bad in the fridge. You don't make good choices. The same thing can happen when you are just out of a committed relationship. You aren't sure what you need, so you have no discretion, dating anyone available. Before going out into the dating fray, sit down and make a "grocery" list to safeguard against "impulse buys."

Think about those qualities in a man that make you happy. Don't only focus on surface qualities, such as looks or job. Evaluate his morals and values, his communication skills, his capacity to love, give, and feel. What does he consider important: friends? money? his car? Remember, the goal is to find your soul mate, a man with whom you can deeply bond, who shares similar feelings, values, and interests. You are looking for a person you can easily talk to, someone to have fun with. Once you have a clear advance understanding of what you really want on the inside, what's on the outside won't be so distracting.

Your Mission Statement

If you were looking for a car, would you buy the first one you saw, or would you look around carefully and research all the options to find the right one? Of course, with big-ticket items, you study the market and comparison shop. Don't you agree a potential mate is worth a lot more than a $20,000 car? All too often, women spend more time analyzing which shopping options are available than what they desire and need in a mate. Choosing a mate is "purchasing" your future. You can trade in the car or hand down your clothes, but it's not so easy to discard an incompatible guy after you've invested your heart and time.

Before you make impulsive, uneducated decisions, devise a mission statement. Like every serious goal in your life, you need to get yourself a framework from which to operate. Analyze what you want before you let the natural evolution of the relationship take over. This is an essential element in getting control of your love life.

Making the List

Sit down and make a list of every conceivable quality you would like a man to have. Be realistic. This project should take some time. Remember—this is your life! The list will help you to choose the men you date and eventually your potential mate. What qualities should he have? What would you like from him? What do you need from him? And . . . what can you give to him? This is a framework within which to consider your options. The more you date the essential elements will crystalize.

Once you reach the supermarket with your grocery list you'll always see a constant flow of new products you never imagined existed. Remember, you want a man, not a Ken doll! Make your list flexible enough to allow for variation and to recognize opportunities when you see them. Although he might not fit the exact criteria on the list, he could still be very special. Your list will change as you evolve or as you meet great guys who show you new qualities to cherish. Let yourself be surprised! Be open to how he might excel in areas that aren't even on your list.

I expect that every woman wants a man who is honest, trustworthy, loyal, faithful, and kind. If you are having trouble thinking of other attributes, here's a list that you can adapt and make your own.

Character	Absolutely Necessary	Desirable	Not Important
Responsible			
Spiritual			
Religious			
Humble			
Confident			
Flexible			
Fair			
Respectful			
Intelligent			
Intellectual			
Interested in Culture			
Good with Children			
Humanitarian			
Not Materialistic			
Positive			
Gentle			
Appreciative			
Sensitive			
Giving			
Adventurous			
Calm			
Philosophical			

	Absolutely Necessary	Desirable	Not Important
Background			
Similar Socio-economic Background			
Compatible Religion			
Similar Education Level			
Nice Family			

	Absolutely Necessary	Desirable	Not Important
Personality			
Good Communicator			
Good Self-esteem			
Likes to Laugh			
Good Tempered			
Charming			
Not Flirtatious			
Independent			
Spontaneous			
Sense of Humor			
Affectionate			
Able to Listen Well			

Habits/Lifestyle	Absolutely Necessary	Desirable	Not Important
Musical			
Likes Learning New Things			
Adventuresome			
Good Mannered			
Knows How to Cook			
Domestic			
Neat			
Organized			
Likes to Dance			
Likes to Sing			
Likes to Read			
Likes to Travel			
Athletic			
Likes Outdoors			
Likes Animals			
Doesn't Smoke			
Meditates			

	Absolutely Necessary	Desirable	Not Important
Interpersonal			
Likes to Do Things for Others			
Thoughtful			
Giver			
Easy to Talk to			
Likes My Family			
Likes My Friends			
Has Nice Friends			
Respects Me			
Understanding			
Shares Tasks			
Cozy			
Adores Me			
Enjoys Sex			
Knows How to Compromise			
Wants Marriage			
Wants Children			

	Absolutely Necessary	Desirable	Not Important
Appearance			
Good-looking, Attractive			
Has a Good Body			
In Good Health			
Smiles Often			
Wants to Be Attractive for Me			
Similar Dress Style			
Age			

After you complete your list, think back to the worst relationship you ever had and see how that man fits into your list. He probably rates very low in the "Absolutely Necessary" category. From now on, when you meet a guy who does not have most of the Absolutely Necessary items on your list, think about why you would want to get into a serious relationship with him. This man is not worth a substantial investment of your time or emotions. With this advance wisdom, you can then limit your involvement to casual dating. If you jump into a relationship while compromising on important issues or anticipating a miraculous change in your man, you may end up painting yourself into a corner. Many women fall into the trap of having invested so much time, energy, and love into a relationship that they are willing to ignore their own doubts in order to save their "investment." Be assured, you will never change the fundamental essence of someone's character.

Identifying Men's Developmental Stages

You might not be ready to consider marriage for years, or you may be ready now. Either way, you need to know where he's at to eliminate potential heartbreaks before they happen. We need to lead with our heads and let our hearts follow. What you're looking for is going to vary according to your age and experience. A twenty-year-old's ideal will be completely different than a thirty- or forty-year-old's. Your perspective and values can evolve and change dramatically even over a few years. Likewise, men's interests and needs change depending on where they are in the life cycle.

For example, men are often told not to marry until they are at least thirty. They may pass up amazing girls due to this programming, but it's as if a light switch goes on at their thirtieth birthday. "Aah! I'm thirty years old, I need to start thinking about who to spend the rest of my life with." If his temperament and nature is consistently relationship-oriented he will reach this stage somewhat earlier. However, age can provide reliable clues to understanding how men think and why they act as they do at various times in their lives. If you understand what stage they're in, it will be easier to anticipate their moves and thoughts.

Boys in Their Twenties

These boys are in the hunting, gathering, and experimenting stage. The twenties are full of many opportunities to easily meet scores of single people and create new friends. The single scene at this stage is buzzing, and men generally go out to bond, drink, and hang out with their buddies. If a girl approaches a guy in his twenties, his defenses don't go up. He's open and ready to be engaged in conversation. During this stage, men tend to focus on their careers and their carnal instincts, although not necessarily in that order. Steve, a twenty-three-year-old composer and songwriter, professed, "Dude, there's short-term goals and the abyss. I'm looking no further than the next three months."

The twenty-something male is not usually looking for his lifetime mate. Still unsure of who he is and what he wants, he doesn't have the time or focus needed to build a long-term relationship. If he has a chaotic life and is not settled in his job, he will usually feel years away from marriage. (And keep in mind that some men never get out of this chaotic, unsettled stage.)

The twenties can be broken down into further subcategories:

The Immortals (20–23 years old) Everything is new and exciting. Life is sampled in gulps. They don't want to miss anything. With one foot still firmly planted in collegiate life, the pressure of real life hasn't yet reared its ugly head. He's carefree and has time on his hands; be aware that he's probably looking for a warm body, not a relationship. Generally, quantity takes precedence over quality. Relationships tend to burn bright and fizzle fast. Favorite pastime: meeting the guys five nights a week to drink and/or watch the game. Favorite thought: what it would be like to have sex with every new girl he sees.

The Straddlers (24–26 years old) Caught between two worlds, the straddler's freedom is on the wane and responsibility looms ahead. His career and the real world have had a sobering influence. Afraid of marriage, but not of love, the straddler finds that a great girl and a relationship are appealing, but his career and finances are not yet on solid ground, and he is generally not ready to think "forever" (nor should he be). This doesn't mean you should discount men in their twenties who haven't made their professional mark yet. If such a man is right for you in all other respects, he can be a marvelous partner with whom to grow and develop.

The Jockeys (27–29 years old) In a race to get ahead, the jockey operates at full throttle using his peak energy to his advantage and emerging as a force in his own right. Business din-

ners and work-related functions take precedence over party-
ing with the boys. As Brad, an ambitious twenty-nine-year-old
working at a real estate consulting firm, put it, "I can't keep up
with my friends and get into work the next day. My career is
my priority, and now that my student loans are paid off, I feel
I'm truly my own master." He has more stability to offer a partner. However, he now has the ways and means to enjoy the
good life. So he may want to taste the fine wine as well as the
women the world has to offer before settling down.

Men in Their Thirties

Although still open, the man in his thirties tends to be more
cautious than those in the carefree twenties. There are still lots
of single early thirties men out on the town. He goes out not to
get drunk, but rather to relax after work with friends or (still!)
to watch the game. Having had more life experience, love af-
fairs, and rejections, he is more sensitive and careful. He has
developed ideas about what he wants and how women operate and think. He is still focused on building his career, but he
feels a sense of financial accomplishment and is often ready to
take on the responsibility of marriage and children. He may be
tired of the dating routine and is less likely to pass up a great
relationship. His friends are getting married, leaving him no
one to play with. Professional happiness and success allow
him to open up and connect with someone. Now that he most
likely lives on his own (no more roommates), he is secure in his
own life and ready to build a long-term relationship. Dave's
view was, "I just had to get it out of my system. There were so
many new and exciting possibilities to explore in my twenties,
I didn't want to miss out on anything. Now, at thirty-two, I feel
much calmer, more at peace. I want to build something real,
something lasting."

Men in their Forties

Men in their forties are probably not going to have much interest in the traditional bar scene. The typical places these men

frequent (cigar bars, piano bars, after-work spots) will also be full of their married friends and coworkers. They are more cautious—if a girl initiates a conversation, all the alarms go off: What does she want? It's up to you to decipher whether this man is a chronic bachelor or intends to get married someday. (If their fathers married late in life, sons often follow.) Is he recovering from divorce? Has he had a series of long relationships that didn't work out for one reason or another, or is he on the scene bouncing from one short-term situation to another? He may have been single so long, he's lost the ability to compromise or lacks the flexibility necessary to include someone else in his lifestyle. Or he simply might be waiting for the right fit. The man in his forties has definite perks: he is usually more stable in his career, relaxed in himself and knowledgeable about what he wants in a woman. Because of this, he is often well prepared to commit to the woman he loves.

Categorizing Men

Many educated professional women look forward to someday being more traditional, stay-at-home moms. Whatever your choice may be someday, it's good to know your mate will support you.

As you do your "market research," chatting with each eligible man you meet, get a preliminary fix on his deep-down attitudes on modern women versus traditional roles. Does he resent the independent, equal-in-every-way woman and secretly long for an old-fashioned girl? Does he expect to take charge? Is he likely to resent the career demands of a professional woman? Or does he want a woman to be his equal? Try and ascertain if you're on the same wavelength on these important issues, and you'll save yourself a lot of trouble. This advance knowledge will keep you from yielding your heart unwisely, only to realize months or years later that a serious relationship was never in the cards. Know what you want from the men you meet and what they're likely to want from you.

This is easy if you know his life stage. When it comes to settling down, timing is everything.

Sweet Young Thing (SYT)

The SYT has the qualities you're looking for: he's great company, but he's not looking for Ms. Right yet. Younger men find the sophistication and independence of an older woman alluring and exciting. The SYT comes with a bevy of positives; he's enthusiastic, appreciative, inquisitive, relaxed, spontaneous, and passionate.

An SYT may still be in school or starting to focus on his career, but he's still carefree. Climbing the career ladder has not yet become a top priority, so he has more time to focus on you! Make sure you put it all in perspective, though. These are cute boys (CBs) who you can have lots of fun with, but odds are that this is a short-term relationship. Don't get your heart set on one unless you're willing to put in a lot of time. Remember, unless he's unusually mature, most SYTs want to sow their wild oats before they settle down.

Be prepared to pick very casual, inexpensive restaurants or to go dutch. Don't put him in the poorhouse. I would rather laugh and have fun with a great SYT than to be bored stiff over a six-course meal with a ROF (Rich Old Fart). Besides, teaching, being a mentor, and helping young minds flourish is a public service!

Midrange (MID)

This is the most dangerous category. Too good to ignore but not what you need, they may only possess seven of your ten "must-have" qualities, i.e., you don't want to spend years waiting for the missing qualities to develop. The goal here is to avoid any two- or three-year relationships that should never have started. Randy was the star of the football team. He was gorgeous and gregarious, and I was swept off my feet. Even though he was faithful and loving, two issues surfaced. He enjoyed drinking every weekend at parties, and I didn't. A few hours into a party, after he'd had one too many, I may as well have been talking to the plants. He also showed no interest in ever leaving his small clique to explore the world. As great as his many attributes were, I would have been stifled and lonely long-term.

The term "midrange" can also apply to age and how ready a man is to be in a committed relationship. MIDs fall into the "almost but not quite ready to settle down" category. In New York City, this age of woe is around twenty-seven, twenty-eight. They have started to do well in their careers, have paid off most of their debts, and can easily walk the walk and talk the talk of a man ready for a serious commitment. The problem is, he often has a little voice telling him, "Now that you can finally afford to take women out, you should enjoy yourself for a few years!" Many longtime steadies get the heave-ho so these midrangers can make the most of their situation.

Don't let the MID men mislead you. Before you invest too much in one, be very careful. Remember, the more you invest emotionally, the harder it will be to leave. Don't dream these attachments will be permanent if the reality is that they should only be regarded as temporary. Proceed with caution! Guys like this may think they're more ready than they actually are.

Transitional Man (TM)

The transitional man helps us get from point A to point B. We've done little or no homework on him, and we don't care to. Maybe we just broke up with someone and this TM was in the right place at the right time when we needed someone, anyone, to comfort us. Once we are strong and on our feet again, we will probably look for someone completely different. After one heartbreak, the last thing you need is another. Have fun with your TM, but remember that you fell into this. He's not meant to be there forever.

Potential Future Husband (PFH)*

Long-term candidates. They've seen it all, may have done it all, and, most important, they now want something meaningful and lasting. A PFH is happy, confident, and strong within himself. He's sown his wild oats and would like to find a wonderful woman with whom to share his life. He seems to have those qualities absolutely necessary to ensure your happiness. You've done your homework, and your mind and heart agree that he's possibly the one.

If you meet a PFH who seems to be exactly what you're looking for, but he isn't jumping at the chance to date you, make him your friend. You never know what's going on in his life or when those circumstances will change. Joe, a successful analyst on Wall Street, was to be transferred to Boston in three months with his job. Because of his move he was reluctant to begin any romantic relationships. Melissa agreed to keep things platonic, and they developed a friendship. Two weeks after he was settled in his new job, Joe let her know that he'd like to see her romantically.

Chronic Bachelors

They are revisiting their early twenties (or never left them) and are still more interested in quantity than quality. These are usually confirmed bachelors over forty-five who are just looking for fun. They may have been married but have no interest in getting hitched again. Check these men out very carefully before proceeding. They'll often shower you with the material symbols of love, but have no intention of giving up their hearts. Their walls have been built so high you'd need dynamite to dislodge them.

Afraid of a real relationship with a woman close to their age, some tend to date only younger women in an attempt to relive their youth. And the younger the better, because these

*If marriage is not on your radar screen for years to come but finding a great significant other is, you can replace PFH with "Potential Future Boyfriend."

men know that twenty-something women will not pressure them for a commitment. In general, unlike PFHs, chronic bache-lors are jaded—they've seen it, had it, done it, been there, and are *still* there.

Divorced or Separated (DOS)

There are, of course, many divorced men on the singles scene. Some want to dive right back into marriage again, others may be gun-shy. Plusses: He has learned from his mistakes. Dealing with the pain of a divorce may have made him more compassionate and empathetic. He has no delusions or roman-tic fantasies about living day-to-day with someone. Minuses: An ex-wife, guilt over leaving his children, unresolved feel-ings, and anger. Does he have baggage that would put Imelda Marcos to shame? Warning: If you're putting all of your energy into helping a man through his divorce, this may not be an equi-table relationship. You could be doing all the giving. When he no longer needs your help, will he be there for you? How will he and the relationship change? Be cautious until after the pa-pers are signed. You need to see if he is really capable of being there for you, too.

In love with a recently separated man and seeing his pain, my friend Debbie moved in to help. She loaned him money, cooked for him, took care of his children, and supported him emotionally through this difficult time. The divorce finally came through, freeing up his assets—and his ego. Within two weeks he announced he was dating others. Although Debbie was there in his darkest moments, he abandoned her once he was back on track.

Unhealthy Choices

An unhealthy choice is any guy who plays into your own weakness, who pushes your buttons. Why do girls hold onto these loser guys? Rooted in low self-esteem, she convinces herself that this man is who she wants to be with. Either she thinks she passionately needs him, or she craves his need for her. Here are some classic loser guys you should avoid.

Bad Boys

Some women are attracted to men with bad reputations and then are surprised when they become his latest victim. "I know he's done that to four other girls, but our relationship is different. He'll never do it to me—I'm special." Don't be so sure! Be smart and look before you leap. Don't be so quick to dismiss warnings from others. Their experiences can often be valuable lessons.

Someone Else's Husband

Don't waste time on a man who is wearing a wedding ring by falling for the classic lines "My wife doesn't understand me"; "We haven't had sex in over a year"; "I plan to leave her soon." Your involvement here can hurt many others. Remember, this man made a vow. Why date unavailable men when there are so many single ones out there? Don't mess with your own fate or karma by interfering with or breaking up someone else's relationship.

Men Like Dad (When Dad Is Bad News)

It's one thing to pick a man like your dad because he truly is Mr. Wonderful, but maybe your father was different. Maybe he wasn't around much. Maybe he worked long hours and getting his attention and love was a challenge. Many women choose men who, like their fathers, reinforce feelings of inadequacy. Perhaps your new love is a workaholic, preoccupied, uncaring, reserved, selfish, or afraid of intimacy. Incapable of giving you the love you need and deserve, he may fulfill a familiar pattern and provide a certain comfort level. But this kind of relationship is unhealthy and interferes with your ability to achieve intimacy. Are you subconsciously looking for and finding men who duplicate your father's inadequacies? Be aware of this pattern so you can change it.

Takers

Takers are selfish with their time, affection, and money. When they do give, it's usually just enough to get what they want. When Jane was dating Phil, her friends and family noticed that she was not her usual bouncy, giving self. She wasn't there for her friends and family the way she used to be. Phil was tapping out her generosity. Tripping over herself to please him, Jane felt less and less good about herself as Phil demanded more and more. Relationships should always be a balance of give and take.

Analyze your partner on the give/take scale. Does he take pleasure from giving physically, emotionally, and materially? Does he do little things just to let you know he cares? Do you get appreciation or recognition from him? Look closely at how he extends himself to other people. Does he give with his heart or with his wallet? If you have money, it's a cinch to give it. It's another thing to make the effort and give with your heart, time, and mind.

No matter how much you give, a taker will always seem to need more. Takers have a habit of being negative; they feel that people—the world in general—owe them. Don't get caught in the trap of trying to fill a leaky bucket. Takers pull you down. If the flow of energy and support is constantly from you to him, you will wake up one day like Jane, to find you've lost your focus and your optimism. There will be very little joy left in giving or in the relationship, and worst of all, you might start to believe you don't deserve any better.

Sugar Daddies (Wealthy Men You Don't Love)

If your main objective is money, ask yourself seriously what this will cost you down the road. There is truth in the old saying, "If you marry for money, you will earn every cent of it." We are bombarded on a daily basis with new things to buy.

Money does, to a certain extent, provide freedom, but marrying a man for money is like walking willingly into prison. You're shutting down an important dimension of yourself by agreeing to a loveless companionship. Many women give up emotional satisfaction and happiness for financial security, forgetting that nothing feels worse than compromising your integrity. Some men feel that when they have money, they can buy a wife or a girlfriend—"a trophy"—whom they can control. If she's a good girl and stays in line, she gets her allowance. Being subservient is not a price worth paying. Some women think they're being practical by putting money first. Don't convince yourself that staying in a bad relationship for the lifestyle is worthwhile. A good relationship is always worth more than money can buy.

Cynthia's entrepreneurial husband, Malcolm, made a fortune in technology. Seduced by his summer home, boats, travel, and the status and security this lifestyle provided, she once confided in a friend, "I'm signing up for that program!" On the outside it looked like a magical life, but she soon felt more like a child than a spouse. When she thought of leaving, she was trapped by her own expectations. How could she live without her Kate Spade bags and her weekly pedicure and facial?

In the blinding search for these trappings, some forget that the things that matter are our values and the people we love. Money might help make life easier, but it did not help Cynthia find happiness or love, nor did it protect her from unhappiness or divorce. It's a seductive illusion, like a drug—the "money high" is superficial and man-made. It would be a tragedy to dismiss a great guy who falls short financially but has all the other credentials you're looking for. Cynthia, now divorced, learned that it's far better to be with someone you love than to be wealthy, lonely, and sad with someone you don't.

Remember, what makes a guy great is not his Mercedes or his beautiful townhouse. A great man is honest, big hearted, and treats others with respect and kindness. When you look him in the eye, he inspires your trust and love.

Personality Flaws

Knowing which qualities to avoid is just as important as knowing what you want. Men are like diamonds: their sparkle may hide unattractive flaws. Small flaws can be accepted and overlooked; for example, he could be stubborn, lazy, or messy, but still be a real gem. But a bad temper or an addiction should immediately indicate that your man is not simply a "diamond in the rough."

Listen to your instincts. It's easy to get into bad situations by ignoring that warning voice in your head. Don't think you can change him. Have you ever heard the expression, "Why teach a pig to sing? It will only frustrate you and annoy the pig." I don't know about you, but I don't want my partner to be my life project. If he changes, he will change because *he* wants to—but this is rare. What you see is what you get, with few exceptions. If there is a quality of high priority on your list and he doesn't exhibit it, he probably never will.

Go out and find a man that has the qualities you want and make sure, *before* you allow yourself to fall in love, that he doesn't have any of the following:

Alcohol and Drug Addicts

Addicts are notorious for covering up their addiction, but certain symptoms are warnings that a man has a substance abuse problems. Does he have unexplained physical symptoms: shaky hands, sweating, vomiting—excess energy or exhaustion? Does he go through sudden mood changes, becoming loud and angry and then quiet and depressed? Does he suddenly disappear for periods of time without giving you an explanation? Have you uncovered drug paraphernalia or stashed alcohol in his home or car?

Often an alcohol or drug addiction stunts the emotional and psychological development, especially if they've been abusing since their teens. If someone is an addict, they are an addict first and in a relationship second. They can function but nevertheless are seriously damaged by their problem. Trying to save them yourself without help is going to be impossible. They must get to AA or a drug rehabilitation center. Addicts need professional help.

Physical and Mental Abusers

Many women abused by husbands or lovers remain with their abusers—out of fear, loyalty, shame or even guilt. Whatever the reason, we all know this is crazy. A healthy man wants a woman who's strong and capable, with self-esteem and confidence. He would never turn her into a victim by abusing or hurting her.

If you're in a relationship with an abusive man, you both have a problem. Realistically, the only problem you can solve is your own. You have rights over your own body, your life, your dreams. Why would you choose to give any of these to somebody who will hurt you? It may not be readily apparent, but it's as much about you as it is about him.

A lot of women who tolerate physical and mental abuse feel helpless, either financially or emotionally. Having invested so much in the relationship, they feel shackled or trapped, because he's the breadwinner. A woman who has control of her own life is less vulnerable to these snares. That's why it is so important to make the right choices early on, so you won't wake up five years down the road and find yourself in an abusive relationship with the father of your children. Make active, healthy choices for your life from day one. You do deserve better. Finding a support group can provide tremendous momentum to propel you out of these unhealthy situations, or you may consider counseling or a personal growth program such as the Hoffman Quadrinity Process.* Never be embarrassed to acknowledge the truth—stand up for yourself!

The bottom line is, nobody has the right to hurt other

*For more information call 1-800-506-5253 or visit them on the Web at www.hoffmaninstitute.org

people, even if they've been hurt themselves. *There is no excuse for abuse!* This goes for emotional and verbal abuse, too.

Control Freaks

Phil constantly puts Jane down in front of their friends. He's the kind of man that makes her feel she's not good enough. Something is always wrong, and she must change to please him. If she gets positive attention from others, he's sure to criticize her in some way. To gain control, he tries to alienate her from her friends and family. By rearranging the facts and repeating things others say out of context, Phil puts false ideas in her head in order to make her question other people's motives. Phil says things like, "Your best friend is always hitting on me"; "Your friend Samantha is saying negative things about you behind your back"; or "I think your family is trying to break us apart."

This kind of man is a savvy manipulator who tries to erode a woman's self-esteem so she requires his approval to make any decision or even to feel good about herself. The control freak wants to control you, because it makes him feel manly and strong. He puts you down to make himself feel better. He knows that when he does, you'll jump through hoops to regain his approval. If you give in to this kind of behavior, he'll soon control everything you do and how you feel. You'll believe that you're not smart enough or aware enough to do things on your own. By letting him criticize you and make your decisions for you, you are allowing him to treat you as his subordinate, not his equal.

You deserve a man who supports you, not one who is trying to break you. Even if he loves you, his behavior is aimed at destroying your confidence and should not be tolerated. Consider the fact that no matter what you do, the Phils of this world will always find something to criticize. Stand your ground early on. Don't set up a pattern where he learns he can take advantage of you. Respect him, but don't let him control you. Make decisions on your own and as a team. If he continues his controlling behavior, run away and don't look back!

Compulsive Liars

Beware of the compulsive liar/con man who lures people into liking and trusting him by making promises he never intends to keep. If something doesn't seem right to you, if it just doesn't ring true, then find out the real story before you get involved. Patty met a charming Frenchman and, without knowing anything about him, started a whirlwind affair. The relationship got serious. They began flying back and forth between Paris and Los Angeles every month to see each other. Patty didn't think twice about his small Paris apartment; she knew he had most of his things at his large summer house in the country. He met her family and talked about their future together. A year raced by. She was in love with him and was waiting for him to pop the question. Finally, she started to wonder why she had trouble reaching him at his home number and why she had never met any of his family or friends. Feeling suspicious, she hired a private investigator in France. It only took one day to find out that this man was planning to marry his fiancée, who was also the mother of his child. Most of what he'd told her had been lies.

If she had been more alert to the signs, she would have figured it out much sooner by herself. Not only had there been several nagging signals she had forced to the back of her mind, she was given a direct warning which she ignored. Months before, this man's secretary had told her, "You're too good for him. He is not a good person. Pack your bags and go back to America and forget about him." Instead of trying to find out more, she told the boyfriend what the secretary had said. If someone is trying to warn you, pay attention. Find out the facts for yourself. Don't always assume that the person offering the warning has an ulterior motive or that you know better.

When you're blinded by the chance of a new romance or a potential marriage, it is often easier to deny the signs than to face the truth. You don't want to hear or believe anything that jeopardizes the security of your relationship, the security of a precious dream. Obviously, you have to evaluate your source: Is his secretary a big gossip who loves to cause trouble? Be aware of the clues and listen to old and trusted friends. And if you don't have his home phone number after dating for months, wake up! It's because he lives with another woman.

Ragers

Bad tempers destroy the spirit. People who throw their anger around like fireballs use it as a technique to manipulate and oppress. This may be high drama, but it is not conducive to a healthy relationship. It forces the other person always to be on their guard, hypercareful and even secretive. How can you ever feel comfortable or safe when you constantly have to fear his anger or displeasure? Ragers need total control over their environment. If you've seen him scream and yell at or about others, don't think it won't be directed at you one day. And don't think you can change him. This behavior might work on the floor of the stock exchange, but it's extremely detrimental to any relationship. When you're trying on a new dress and you see that it doesn't fit, you immediately know you aren't going to buy it and you move on. Do the same with men. If you know this guy has a serious personality flaw, don't get into a relationship with him—*get out!*

Remember

- Don't lose your IQ because he's gorgeous or great in bed.
- Know what you want before you start looking and make sure it exists.
- Draw up a list of what you're looking for and make sure it's in line with what you have to offer.
- Do your research—find out who he *really* is.
- Remember that he may have the right qualities, but if he's at a different stage of life than you, it probably won't work.

- Choosing a man solely on his financial status is an unhealthy choice.
- No matter how much you love someone, you can't change them to save the relationship. The only person you can change is yourself.

6

Hunting

Marriage is a great institution, but I am not ready to be institutionalized yet.

—Mae West

Early Saturday morning Katie woke up with that delicious "got the whole weekend ahead of me" feeling. She thought of all the things she wanted to do as the coffee brewed and she pulled out her Rollerblades. When she got to "tonight" she decided to call her best friends, Anna and Louise. Maybe they could hang out, watch a movie, whatever.

"Hey, Anna, hope I didn't wake you and your bed warmer."

"Ha, ha, very funny! No you didn't, and the puppy's at my parents' house for the weekend. Listen, I have plans for us," Anna said with a note of mischief. "I spoke to Louise, and Dave's going out with the boys to watch the game, so the three of us, my dear, are going hunting!"

Katie laughed. "I'm a bit scared to ask what that means exactly."

"Just get ready for girls' night out, and I'll be over at eight," Anna said before she hung up.

As Katie bladed out the front door, she felt a surge of exhilaration.

Becoming a Huntress

One of the best things about being single is the freedom you possess: You are free to meet new people, free to try different social groups, and free to experience a variety of lifestyles. But how do you do it? How do you meet people if you're single? How do you decide whom to meet and where to go? In other words, how do you take charge of your own life? Taking charge is what the hunting phase is all about. Instead of sitting around waiting for a prince to sweep you off your feet, you are out there initiating encounters, introducing yourself to people, making things happen—having fun! Remember, if you trigger the encounter, you can control it.

Hunting is deciding to take a macro view of the dating landscape, to adopt a big-picture perspective on the opportunities available—to actively adopt a bird's-eye view. Instead of being a mouse and only noticing and reacting to people in your immediate vicinity, choose to be an eagle soaring over the landscape, scouring the terrain.

Hunting is a frame of mind. Now that you know what qualities and values you're looking for, it's time for the action stage; taking a stand and affirming that you can create your own opportunities, expand your horizons, and shape your own destiny.

The Hunt

The reality is, if you want a great man, you'll have to go out and get him. Time is too precious to sit passively waiting for life to happen, hoping that a special someone will pick you out of the crowd. It's time for *you* to do the choosing. No one knows better than you what kind of partner you want. So gather up your courage and start hunting.

Harold, a twenty-seven-year-old stockbroker, uses the "shotgun approach" to pick up women. He hits on every girl in the room and finally one says "yes." He's simply on the make. If he's looking for anything, it's a warm body, not a real relationship. If you can understand how the Harolds of the world think—and refuse to fall prey to them—you're one step ahead. Thankfully there are other men who would love to find a great girl like you and begin a wonderful relationship. The men you want to meet, the ones who are caring, hardworking, and serious about creating a future, are out for a drink with friends or in the park playing football or Rollerblading. They may be quieter, shy men who don't go out as much and are unlikely to leave their friends to talk to a woman, let alone approach a group of women sitting together. They're not nerds or klutzes, but merely guys who would love to meet a compatible, genuine woman but don't know how to take that first step.

Why Go Hunting?

Wherever you go, you're not always going to find what you're looking for. There's no money-back guarantee. But, by being out there, you'll eventually eliminate what you don't want and, possibly when you least expect it, find what you do want. This means interacting with as many single men as possible. Give yourself more options, and remember, you can always say no.

Being single, unattached, and free is not something to fear; it's something to experience and cherish. Your goal is to get good at being single, to enjoy it as much as you will someday enjoy being with a wonderful man in a committed relationship. Being single is a valid and valuable life stage that can provide you with some of the most enriching moments of your life. Don't waste your time crying and wishing you were in a relationship. Now that you've formulated ideas on the types of men you want to spend time with, go out, have fun, and enjoy some of the available, smart, great men on this planet! Use this time to discover yourself and the world and to create your own life. Your happiness is not on hold until you find "the one" and that elusive ring is on your finger. If you're busy and fulfilled, enjoying the present, you'll be the type of woman men want to meet. They will want to be a part of your fabulous life!

Like most of her friends, Kathryn, a twenty-three-year-old artist, would focus on one man until the relationship ran its course. Imagining that there could be quality in quantity was contrary to everything she'd been taught. Instead of immediately attaching herself to the next guy she met, I suggested she try going out and looking for a whole bunch of fun guys to date, to think of it as just another activity she'd be adding to her life. Kathryn set herself a goal, to become an active huntress and have a lot of fun doing it. She made a commitment to herself, "I am not going to look for marriage or a serious relationship for the next eight months. Instead, I'll focus on going out and creating as many opportunities as possible."

Think about it. When you choose a school, you apply to more than one and then take the best offer. It's just good common sense that when you are choosing a mate, the more options you examine, the more screening you do, the better your end result will be. When Kathryn truly made this commitment to change her attitude, men immediately sensed it. They no longer felt pressured. She acknowledged, "What did I have to lose? By following these new dating guidelines I had way more men to choose from. They were swarming like bees to honey."

Hunting provides you with knowledge. After eight months of hunting, you'll:

- know yourself much better: who you are and what you want.
- have seen for yourself what's out there.
- have lots of men to choose from.
- know that you *can* have a great life being single and, as a result, be less likely to put up with a destructive relationship.

What Do You Take on a Hunting Expedition?

Attitude

Whether your expedition will be to a conference, beach, sailing, skiing, or a bar, these same techniques apply. Have fun!

Look at hunting as a sport like shopping—it's a really fun thing to do, even if you don't buy anything! Don't start by saying, "Oh no, I hate walking into a crowded room." You have to give it a chance. Don't think, "I can't handle the thought of going out to bars or parties and getting pushed and shoved." You will automatically put up your defenses and be right back where you started: lonely. There are so many excuses you can make: "Everyone is too old or too young." "It's not sophisticated enough." "I can't afford it." "It's too noisy." Instead of looking at the hunting expedition as something difficult or unpleasant, look at it as an adventure. You're going to see what the single scene is all about. Don't let the fear of the unknown stop you from actively creating opportunities in your life. If you do, you are giving fear more power than you give yourself. Be courageous—challenge yourself!

No one wants to be with someone whose only goal in life is to find a spouse. I wouldn't want to hang out with girlfriends who feel this way. I go out with friends who want to have a good time and enjoy being in the here and now. Men feel the same way. Desperation is weakness, and weakness is not fun or attractive. Paula, a pretty, twenty-eight-year-old fashion executive, hates going out to bars, parties, or clubs. When I see her out at a party or a business function, she stands aloof, sipping her drink, looking unhappy, uncomfortable, and unapproachable. She always leaves early and alone—and yet she's constantly talking about how much she wants to get married and have children. Consumed with living in her dream world, Paula is missing the present and the chance of making a fabulous future happen. On the other hand, her friend Lilly makes time before every social outing to reconnect with her self-worth, positive energy, and confidence. Despite being very overweight, she has a great time attracting quality people into her life every time she goes out. It just goes to show that attitude is a crucial ingredient in the magical mix of success. Your outlook will determine how you feel and this affects how everyone else you come in contact with reacts to you.

Jason, a successful thirty-six-year-old entrepreneur, put it simply: "All men appreciate optimistic, approachable, confident women. Every guy I know wants to feel a woman sees something unique in him and wouldn't date just any guy that came along." Dating, and then choosing between a number of guys, makes both you and your partner feel the confidence of your choice. One of the things that destroys even good relationships is self-doubt, thinking you might have done better. You're not with him just because you want a relationship. This is the guy. You picked *him*. Become a huntress, rather than just accepting the first man who pursues you!

Friends

Friends are not your competitors but your allies in helping you to find great men. We've been programmed to think of other women as the enemy in our quest for a mate, but they can be beneficial to the hunting process. Plan with a couple of your girlfriends and make every Thursday or Friday your "girls' night out." Three or four is the ideal hunting expedition size. If there are only two of you, men can't ask one of you to dance or have a one-on-one conversation, because you might be reluctant to leave your friend alone. Larger groups are often too hard to organize and too intimidating to men. Mobilize yourself, then help find great guys for your girlfriends, too. Set them up, introduce them around. Who knows, they may just end up with a new boyfriend who has lots of single male friends.

Don't avoid going out with girlfriends who are more attractive or more confident than you because you see them as competition. First of all, everyone's taste is different. Second, they're more likely to act as a magnet, helping to draw people toward you. Third, there are plenty of guys out there and only one of her. By trying to stack the deck in your own favor, you can actually end up hurting yourself by being a bad team player. *Be a good friend first.* Choose hunting companions who are the most fun. Ultimately, happy and enjoyable people attract the same type.

Hunting buddies should be team players. There are advantages to the buddy system and the importance of a good "wingman," as any guy will tell you, is essential. They help extract you from boring conversations and distract his friend so you can zero in on the "target." If you want out, have a pre-arranged code, such as: "Do you have a safety pin?"

For many it's easier to find the confidence to approach someone on a friend's behalf than on your own. If you're a bit shy, a good team player can introduce you in a flattering, positive way to let people know what an amazing, wonderful, talented person you are. "Hi, my name is Jane, and this is Darlene. She's a bit shy tonight but don't let that fool you. She's one of the fastest rising stars in the fabric design business!" or "Tina's the funniest girl you'll ever meet, and Sandy's a really talented writer, she just got her first article published." She can also find out, immediately, from his reaction how interested he is.

I know it might be quite threatening at first but if you have nobody to go out with, and you live in an area where you feel safe and comfortable, try going out alone. Kim, a successful thirty-one-year-old lawyer, always had the excuse that she couldn't round up a hunting buddy. I suggested she summon the courage to fly solo. She reported that "It was easy to make friends with the bouncer and bartenders. I know enough people now that I often drop in after a late night working or on my way home from an early dinner. I already recognize a lot of the same faces. The amazing thing is, I've met some great guys. More than a few admitted to me that being alone is like having a neon sign for them to approach.

Approaching the man you want to meet is much easier when you have a few girlfriends around. However, if he is doing the approaching he may be more likely to try if you don't have any friends along to witness a possible rejection." Don't think for a minute that good girls don't go out without dates. Just be sure you're responsible. This is not the night to drink too much. Make sure the doorman or bouncer sees you safely to your car or taxi.

Proper Hunting Attire

Fair or not, the fact is that men are very visual. Ultimately, it's what's inside that he will fall in love with, but looking good on the outside plays a role. Make an effort with your appearance each time you go out. Remember, the basics still apply: Look neat, pretty, and natural. Don't overdo your perfume, makeup, hair, jewelry, or clothes. Dress to suit your own mood and personality, not to impress him. If you're confident and comfortable, you will radiate. Remember, revealing clothes will more likely than not turn you into the prey rather than the proud huntress. Who wants to spend the whole evening turning away men you're not interested in? It's not productive or fun. You want to narrow the field with your criteria in mind. Opt for the happy medium. Dress for the occasion. Go to clubs in that cute little black dress and to casual bars in your jeans and a sexy T-shirt. But definitely leave your conservative gray flannels and stuffy blazer at home. Looking stylish shows that you respect yourself and the people around you.

Do Your Homework

Be prepared. Nothing is worse than a woman who has nothing to say for herself. Keep up with what's happening in the news or, if you're out of touch, be inquisitive. Have a couple of favorite jokes up your sleeve. If you like bankers and hang out in the places they go, it doesn't hurt to know a thing or two about what they do. Skim *The Economist* or *The Wall Street Journal*. Do some research, learn about the market. So few women really know what these men do all day. Learning a little about the business world not only makes you more interesting but can help in other ways—like guidance on where to invest your own money. Or if you prefer sports-bar types, then watch ESPN and pick a favorite team or player. For some men, finding a woman who can talk about football is a dream come true! Think about how wonderful you feel when you meet someone who listens and can relate to your interests.

There's no need to fake an interest or pretend to be an expert. Just keep in mind that a little knowledge is an empowering way to be alluring and shows you're willing to make an effort to understand his world. And don't be afraid to talk about the things that interest you. If you're confident about what you know and what you have to say you'll never be at a loss or suffer through embarrassingly long pauses in conversation.

Where to Hunt

Bars, Pubs, Clubs

In larger cities, really interesting, nice, normal people (just like you) flood into the local watering hole for a drink after work or for predinner drinks at a restaurant bar with friends. Most, like you, are single and looking to meet someone nice to date. Like shopping at Kmart, there are great bargains if you know what you're looking for. If you need suggestions on where to go, ask hotel concierges what they recommend or check out local publications or handy city guides like Zagat and Sechyl's for suggestions.

If you're not sure where to find an atmosphere or crowd that feels comfortable, call up any bar, ask to speak with the bartenders, manager, or hostess and tell them what you are searching for. "I'd like to find a twenty-to-thirty or thirty-to-forty crowd. Are there any places you can recommend?" And be specific about what you want: sophisticated or casual, noisy or quiet. They'll give you a number of suggestions. If you prefer a sophisticated or mature crowd, ask if there are any cigar bars or piano lounges. Don't forget to ask which nights and at what times each place is "hot," and call these places early before they get too busy.

While dance clubs are great fun, they're usually loud and not conducive to meeting people. Casual bars that serve food are your best bet for meeting quality men and having conversations—as opposed to pickup bars. There's often a fine line between these two. Casual bars tend to have a more down-to-earth feel, and people usually go with groups of friends to hang out. However, if the men look like vultures, and you feel like prey, you're probably in a pickup bar. The great thing about hunting is you can move through the whole room and decide there's no one for you and then leave or stop to talk to exactly who you choose. If you feel uncomfortable or threatened, move to a new spot.

I hear women say, "Well, I live in the suburbs and there is no place to find single men here!" If you do your homework first, in thirty to sixty minutes you can probably drive to an area where you can find places to go. There could be lots of great little pubs, bars, and clubs for you to choose from, plus a plethora of single men!

If it's been a while, your first outing to the bar scene can be quite daunting, if not downright scary. People in crowded bars pushing and bumping you around can be uncomfortable and make you feel claustrophobic. If you think of it as a chore rather than a choice, you probably won't have any fun. But if you give it a chance, you'll be much more likely to enjoy yourself. Your reward for putting your energy into being positive is that you get to have fun, bond with your friends, improve your observation skills, and meet new people (maybe even Mr. Right). Don't get discouraged after one outing. If one place isn't great, try another.

Where Your Interests Are

Put yourself in places where you can meet people who have similar interests. If you like art, go to galleries where you can browse the art and the men. If you love to ride horses, do a little research and find out where the nearest stable is. Go riding there or go to horse shows or a polo match. Study in a coffee shop. Take a cooking class. Attend a conference. Join a book club, a skiing club, a music club. Find a list of charity functions, snoop around, ask questions, and offer to pitch in. Want a man who's good with his hands? Join Habitat for

Humanity. Or borrow a friend's dog and take it for a walk.
Pets are great, they make introductions for you. Pick something that interests you and go!

Kathy, twenty-eight, loved country-and-western line dancing. She went to Denim and Diamonds, a country music club,
and asked a SYT (Sweet Young Thing) to dance (he was
twenty-three). They danced the night away and despite their
five-year age difference, she added him to her dating pool. Before long they fell in love and are now very happily married.
Whenever there is common ground, the ice is already broken
for you, providing a starting point to build on.

On-line

Sandra lived in Indiana; one day she went into a singles
chat room and asked, "Are there any intelligent, spiritual,
lighthearted men over thirty looking for the right woman?"
and met Rob, from New York. After many long, soulful E-mails,
Sandra asked him for his number and called him. She decided
to take a trip to New York City with her girlfriend to meet him.
After a year of long-distance dating, they are now happily
married and living in the city.

Having heard this and other stories of success, I decided to
find out for myself what computer dating was all about. As research, I joined match.com, one of the largest Internet dating
services.* They asked my preference on height, age, religion,
and location. Within my initial qualifications in the New York
area alone, 500 bios popped up. To narrow this down, I decided to use my proactive technique on-line. Instead of only
listing what I had to offer like all the others, I also set up a
questionnaire and sent it to every guy whose bio looked interesting. I listed ten things I was looking for and asked that only
men who were an eight out of ten or above respond. It worked
like a charm; more than eighty men E-mailed back with a photo
hoping to pass my test. Considering my girlfriend had only

*To easily navigate the hundreds of on-line dating services, I suggest www.
xseeksy.com, a porthole to all the best websites.

received six responses in her first two weeks, I knew I was definitely doing something right! After I further narrowed this group down the fun started. I called one of my girlfriends and set up two double blind dates for us each night. We met twenty guys in two weeks!

Here are some ideas if you decide to try this medium. As always, if you're more proactive you'll meet many more men than if you're passive.

- Set up a separate screen name just for your computer dates.
- Don't use any part of your name as your password.
- Instead of just sitting back and waiting for mail, do a search. Make a list of every man who looks interesting and E-mail him your bio.
- Make sure to cut and paste or blind copy so he won't see the others on your list. LOL.
- Insist on getting a photo before you send yours.
- Ask for his number; don't give out yours.
- Don't get too involved or give out too much information until you've exchanged photos.
- Pick two hopefuls and try a double blind date with your girlfriend.
- Pick a comfortable public place for hors d'oeuvres and drinks.
- Set the meeting and departure time in advance. An hour and a half is definitely enough time to know if you're interested in another date.
- You can ask all sorts of questions on the computer that you wouldn't be able to get away with in person. After you've seen his photo and have an idea there may be a match . . . fire away; ask him anything you want to know.

Where the Boys Are

At a dinner with a group of girlfriends, I looked around the table and was struck by the fact that all of them were single except one. They were all gorgeous, smart, successful women, but they all had the same complaint: "Most of the men I meet are jerks or womanizers or on the fast track to nowhere. Where are all the good guys? We see them walking down the street, so we know they exist." It was the million-dollar question.

The answer? Many single men lead sheltered lives. For example, in Manhattan they could be working on the thirty-second floor at a huge law firm or investment bank all day. When they do go out, it's to a nearby pub with their friends from work or to the gym. Meanwhile, they're complaining that they can't meet great girls. What could we do about it? My advice was if the great men can't or won't come to us then we'll go to them! On a warm fall or spring evening, late in the week, the bars in the financial district after work are packed. There are plenty of men unwinding after a long day, ready for some female company. And they must have private parties and after-work get-togethers in pubs or bars. I called friends who worked at these places and asked them to keep me in mind for any of their office social events.

Beat the odds by going to places where men outnumber women. Patricia, a twenty-five-year-old bond trader, says, "I meet more great guys hanging out at the bookstore near my office on Wall Street at lunchtime than most meet in a lifetime. It's all men!" she coos. Sporting events like sailing, golfing, skiing (the odds are fantastic at ski areas—3 or 4 to 1!). I am happy to report that many of my girlfriends are happily dating or have married some of the great guys we met since discovering these untapped sources of dynamic men. If finding Mr. Right is like finding a needle in a haystack, then get out of the haystack and get to the needle factory.

All this may sound a bit difficult, but don't panic! I have a step-by-step method for finding and meeting the men who suit you best in any social situation. The first three steps are outlined below. The fourth and the fifth steps, "The Approach" and "Setting up the Date" are in the following two chapters.

But don't skip ahead; you need to learn how to *spot* the right man before you can *meet* him.

Step One: Put Your Periscope Up

If you look around a room during a social event and study it, you'll usually see small groups of people who came together or who know each other. In general, these groupings are static— they don't change or move from the territory they've staked out. When their friends come back with drinks, they always know where to find their group. Sometimes individuals will walk through all the different groups, but most people stick with their own friends where they feel secure. Wrapped up in their own little world, these groups are often unaware of what's going on around them. If you want to learn how to be good at being single, the first step is to become aware of the people and groups around you.

When Jody walks into a room full of strangers, she feels unsure of herself. "I'm self-conscious because I don't know who the other people are, what dynamics are in play, or how to start meeting people. I feel out of my element." Jody found it hard to believe, that almost everyone else was just as uncomfortable as she was. Even the most gifted politicians don't feel confident when they first walk into a room. Instead of standing there and feeling uncomfortable or sorry for herself, I encouraged her to use this time to change the situation by getting to know it. She went to a quiet corner where she had a good vantage point and watched the room.

By cultivating a genuine interest in learning about her surroundings, Jody turned the focus away from herself and toward others in the room. "The more time I take to observe and understand how the different groups interact, who the individuals are, who the powerful personalities are, and who's controlling the atmosphere, the more comfortable I am. The more I practice, the faster and easier I understand the room." No one can understand these dynamics in the first minute; it takes time. Banish your feelings of insecurity. Use those initial

moments to understand your environment so that you can
then take the next step.

Step Two: Walk Around the Room

If you walk around the room slowly, you'll get an overview
of the entire crowd. After browsing, you can come back to the
best candidate. Don't make any immediate judgments; allow
yourself to take in the whole room and feel comfortable. Your
goal is not to run through at lightning speed, but to move
slowly through the crowd, stopping every five or six feet to
look around, sip your drink, or talk to your girlfriend. The
questions you should be asking yourself are: Who are the fun,
nice, interesting people here? Which men am I drawn to and
why? Who in this room would I choose to spend time with?

Remember, it's useless to spend time watching people if
you can't read them. The more you observe, the stronger your
intuition will be. Study faces, listen to conversations, watch
people interact. As you walk through the room you will re-
ceive many initial impressions: who is catty, friendly, shy,
affectionate, fashionable, or down-to-earth. Use these observations to decide who interests you. The first step is to pick out—
not pick up—the men you're attracted to. Take your time, walk
slowly, and leave no stone unturned. Here are a few hints to
help you remain in control while scoping out the room.

- If you see "Horny Hank" approaching and you're sure
  you don't want to talk, send a clear signal that you're not
  interested. Don't make eye contact, or move to a new location before he has a chance to say hello. If you're not interested, you're not interested. As long as you're not
  rude, no apologies are necessary.
- Avoid getting drawn into a long talk just to be polite,
  unless it's with the man of your choice.
- You can only cross the room twice before everyone no-
  tices. You want to be subtle while you're browsing—
  don't do laps.

- Better to watch from the outskirts of the crowd, rather than risk getting bombarded and overwhelmed in the middle of the scene.
- Accepting a drink = accepting an invitation to talk. In general, never let a guy buy you a drink unless you want to invest fifteen to thirty minutes in him. *Don't waste your valuable time.* Avoid getting stuck—buy your own drink.
- The man who approaches you may be nice, but just not the right person for you. Why should you spend half your night talking with somebody you really don't have that much interest in? Maybe you'll find that you like him, but if you haven't checked out all of your options, it's not an informed decision. You can always come back.
- Use your full sensory awareness and intuition to steer you away from the wrong men and guide you to those with a compatible demeanor. Remember: You're looking for someone with common interests who fits some of your criteria—not somebody to advance your career or pay your bills.
- For goodness sakes, have fun! Even if nothing comes from your adventure, you'll look back on it as a good time shared with friends (or maybe you'll even make a new one).

Step Three: Going In for a Closer Look

After you've done a quick overview, you're ready to check out the eligible candidates. At this point be realistic. If you are looking at a college football player who's 6'4" with three centerfolds next to him, realize that his hands are probably full and don't waste your time. Look for guys who are not already occupied. Someone you feel is in your league, men you like and who you sense may like you. Once you initiate a conversation it would be rude to end it abruptly, so don't jump in too soon. Observe and screen before you approach. Don't stare. Watch him carefully but discreetly for three or four minutes. It doesn't take long. Here are some hints about what to look for.

- How is he talking with others? Is he animated?
- Is he the life of the party or is he quiet and down-to-earth?
- Check for a wedding ring. Don't waste time talking to someone else's husband.
- Ask yourself, Will I feel comfortable talking to him?

Don't spend too much time going in for a closer look. Be bold. Before the five-minute mark, make your move or move on.

Remember

- Instead of waiting to be hunted, be a huntress.
- Beat the odds by going where the boys are rather than waiting for them to find you.

7

·······················

The Approach

·······················

As Katie scanned Pete's, their favorite neighborhood pub, Anna exclaimed, "CB Alert! Just left of the pool table." Katie studied him as he interacted with his buddies. He was attentive, expressive and funny. All good signs. Anna's eyes sparkled with mischief as she grabbed Katie's arm and led her toward the pool table.

In the preceding chapters, I've stressed the importance of taking your life and happiness into your own hands. I've explained the necessity of finding the right places to meet your type and how to identify from a distance those men you'd most like to meet. But how do you actually establish personal contact? How do you start talking to a new person? How do you close the deal and exchange phone numbers?

This is the point where you'll most want to retreat back into familiar passivity. But remember, you've done all the work to get in the right place at the right time. Don't waste it by expecting Prince Charming to read your mind, recognize your hidden charms, pick you out of the crowd, and sweep you off your feet. If you spot a prince only *you* can ensure he spots you, too. Welcome to a world where the Sadie Hawkins dance is in full swing every night.

Overcoming Doubts

Like most women, Marie was used to letting men take the lead. Yet she was rarely meeting or dating anyone. I could sense her nervousness when she asked me, "What will a guy think of me if I approach him? And what if he rejects me?" I asked Bill, a very sought-after bachelor, and he repeated what every man I interviewed had told me. "I never get the wrong idea if I'm approached politely. Confident, outgoing women do not appear desperate for sex or any other kind of attention." Marie's thoughts and doubts were exactly the same as those a man has before he approaches a woman. Bill added "It's scary for anyone to put him or herself on the line and risk rejection. Believe me, most men will be elated that she's taking the responsibility of the approach. Men know how it feels to be shot down by women and will rarely reject someone who makes an effort. After all, I want to know which women are interested in me."

Elizabeth was turning forty. Time seemed more precious to her than ever before. She dreamed of meeting a great guy and starting a family. The problem was that it took a big effort on her part to find the time to go out to meet a new man. "I just don't want to waste my few free hours on a nerve-racking bar outing or first date. I rarely get to see my old friends. I'd rather be home reading a good book or watching my favorite TV show." By not allowing herself to open up, take a risk, and invest some time, she diminishes her own chances.

When you feel shy or uncomfortable meeting new people, remind yourself of the following truths to help you overcome your nervousness:

- You are full of interesting qualities that the right man will be lucky to find!
- Men are struggling through life's challenges just as you are.
- Men are also thinking: I want to make a good impres-

sion; I want people to like and respect me and find me appealing.

- Most men are not only flattered, but relieved, when a woman makes the first move.
- Opportunity often knocks softly; it's up to you to open the door.

Practice Makes Perfect

Marie realized she had very little to lose by introducing herself. To her astonishment people rarely dismissed her. Even though she hadn't met Mr. Forever, every time she approached a new man her confidence and social skills improved. The more she focused and practiced, the more confident she became. Soon she was so comfortable approaching and engaging new people that when she met her soul mate, Gary, she knew exactly how to talk to him. "The old me would never have talked to him. Overcoming the ridiculous stereotype that women can't approach men led me to the greatest relationship of my life."

Introducing Yourself

You have carefully selected a few men in the room with whom you would like to have a conversation. You're now ready to step up to the plate.

There is a fine line between being confident with humor, thoughtfulness, and respect, and being pushy. You don't want to come across as intrusive, offensive, or as someone working the room. It's not about contacts, but about making *connections* with special people. Here are some guidelines.

Wait for the Right Time to Approach

The goal is to join the conversation, not to intrude. Going in for a closer look gives you the chance to notice if he's in a heated discussion or completely focused on one person (not the best time to move in). Be sensitive to his world: Wait until he stops talking, goes to get a drink, or starts looking around the room. Then take a deep breath, remind yourself you have nothing to lose, and walk over, remembering all the while that you are not trying to "pick him up." You're having fun and meeting interesting people.

When it came to meeting men, my friend Andrea was too shy to ever initiate a conversation. For several nights I walked her through the simplicity of it. "I don't know why I thought it would be cheap or tacky of me to approach the man I actually wanted to talk to. It's crazy, I know, but these thoughts stopped me. I just can't believe how easy it is and how unbelievably responsive men are. I've had more dates with men I like in the past few months than I've had in years. Being in control of meeting as many men as I want has changed my life."

Introduce Yourself with Your Name and an Opening Line to Break the Ice

Don't lose the moment. Be as natural and relaxed as possible. Remember your value. Perhaps the lowest-risk strategy with the highest effectiveness is to stand nearby with your friend and ask a general question, directed to the group of guys. "We're trying to figure out the meaning of life over here, do you have any revelations?" "Do you know of any good restaurants in this neighborhood?" "Hi. I'm curious, where did you get those great boots?" If they are laughing, for example, you could say, "You guys look like you're having a lot of fun, can we join in?" If possible, say something funny or interesting with confidence, like "Hi! I'm part of the greeting committee, I'm taking a survey to make sure everyone's having a good time." or "Boy are we lucky girls to stumble upon this group."

For years men have been using tired pickup lines that often make women wince. But old lines turned on men become new again. So go ahead and ask him what a nice guy like him is doing in a place like this. You're bound to spark his interest, attract his attention, and get a smile as he acknowledges your sense of humor. "Has anyone ever told you that you look like (pick the closest movie star match)?" One of my girlfriends stands by her nonthreatening strategy to start a conversation with anyone by asking "Didn't you go to Texas U?" (Insert your own college or hometown school.) Another great way to meet is to ask his opinion about anything under the sun. "Excuse me. We need an objective opinion."

The best introduction is your name and something, anything, that puts you on common ground. It could be as simple as "Wow! It's hot in here," or "I work on the thirty-second floor, too," or "I can't believe we're stuck in here on this gorgeous day." "Does anyone know how the [pick a team] did in the big game last night?" (Sports—a favorite topic for many men.) One time I bumped into a CB (cute boy) at a cocktail party and, noticing his crisply pressed, white Oxford shirt, I said, with a smile, "One big bump in this crowd and you'll be wearing that red wine if you're not careful." He immediately pulled me to a less crowded area and asked me out. Comment on anything you've noticed that's out of the ordinary. But remember, there's no set formula. It doesn't matter what you say to break the ice, if he's interested almost anything will work, if not, nothing will. He may pick up on the conversation, or he may not. If he doesn't, move on.

Making a connection is the key. There are lots of other ways to start a conversation. You can use any excuse to address a situation indirectly and engage him in conversation. I know a girl who spotted a man that she liked at a bar and asked him for a cigarette. They are now happily married and living in England. Another friend of mine met her fiancé by asking a good-looking guy shopping at the computer store for advice on what laptop he thought she should purchase. They exchanged E-mail addresses and she sent him a note: "I would like to take you out for a drink to thank you." The rest was history. How about going to the men's department during a sale?! "Could you help me? I need a man's opinion, do you think my brother would like this?"

For those of you who are feeling a bit more confident, there are other openers. You could try (with a big smile): "This group looks a little too quiet, I thought we should come over to see if we could liven it up" or "My friends and I have done a survey of all of the men at this party/bar/restaurant, and we've unequivocally decided that you're the best-looking man in here. So we're here to award you the prize." "What's the prize?" he asks with a smile. "A drink with us." This always gets a great reaction. Or try, "Are women allowed in this club of good looking guys?" For the bold, it works like a charm. Tip: *All men eat up sincere compliments.* When you compliment his style or something nice about his personality, you disarm him and put him at ease.

Stick to the Positive

Opening comments should not be negative, like "I can't believe what an awful party this is" or "Look at all these conservative people." (It could be his sister's, friend's, or—even worse—his own party!) Find something positive, like "Isn't it great the way Bill takes so much pride in his parties. And everyone seems so nice." Or "I'm so excited to be here to meet Bill's friends. Hi, I'm Kim. How are you?" A positive outlook doesn't just make other people happy, it's a gift to yourself.

Start a Conversation with One of His Friends

You see someone you like. You've caught his eye. You've seen that he's interested, too. But he's not in a circumstance conducive to being approached. What do you do? You can always start a conversation with one of his friends and casually find out about "Steve's" situation. Is that his girlfriend? You can often get a lot of information and perhaps an introduction as well.

If You Love to Dance, Ask Him

You will have a great time dancing, get in your daily aerobic activity, and be on display for other CBs (Cute Boys). Let's face it, there are usually more people watching the dance floor than actually dancing! Most important, you'll establish contact and learn a little more about the man you're interested in. You might find that you have the same taste in music or are compatible dancing partners, which would make a great activity for a possible first date.

Tune in to Where He's Coming from

When guys are together they often speak a language all their own. It's like a secret fraternity. They jostle back and forth, teasing one another, using lots of sarcasm and wit. Most women, however, feel like they've entered a mine field and shrink back from this sort of banter. Rather than feeling reactive and sensitive, step back and enjoy the show or try to join in. If you feel they're operating on a superficial level, find an issue that could connect with their hearts, a local or national issue, involve them emotionally. Men love it when a woman can hit them with a comeback. It puts the communication on a different level. They can now enjoy you as a friend, because this is how they're used to dealing with their male friends. You become less of an alien from a different planet and more of a person they can talk or joke with.

Genuine Warmth and Sincerity Opens Hearts

Remember, you have nothing to lose but a few minutes of your time by approaching someone. If you're friendly and open, guys will feel comfortable, and everyone will enjoy themselves. Men are attracted to women who understand them, women with whom they "click." The key to the "click-quotient" and having others feel comfortable is empathy. If you're genuine, people will open up to you. A woman who is positive, warm, and down-to-earth and has a good sense of humor will be the one who men want to be around. Can you imagine a man saying, "See that cold, aloof woman over there? I just can't wait to put my arms around her." Find and show your femininity, warmth, and kindness.

Give the Green Light

If you're just not ready to approach someone, you can at least give them the green light to approach you. Show him you're interested and approachable by making eye contact or smiling; get "caught" looking at him two or three times. Most men will not risk talking to a girl if she hasn't shown some interest. My friend Mike says, "I would never take the chance of getting shot down unless a girl sent me several large smiles and very clear signals she was interested." So drop the hint. Remember when you were in high school or college, there was an unwritten rule: friends tell each other who likes who, and that's how guys find out so they can make a move. The initial encounter is the hardest thing for both men and women, but if you want control of your life, you must learn to make it happen.

Wait to Ask What They Do

Many men complain that it makes them uncomfortable when the first thing a women asks them is, "What do you do?" Rich explained, "Women think this is a conversation opener or a common denominator. But a man sees it as a dead giveaway of an opportunistic woman evaluating him as a provider." Most people's lives aren't defined by their occupation. Rich added, "I see myself in terms of my hobbies, family, and friends. I wish I'd get asked about these instead. It's way more appealing when a woman focuses on my character and personality." Let him lead by asking what you do first.

Don't Let Brush-offs Get You Down

I find that almost all men are friendly, or at the very least, polite if approached in the right way. From time to time, however, when you extend your hand, it will get bitten. Instead of being hurt, just think of how sad this person's world must be if he is unable or afraid to accept the ray of sunshine you extend to him. If he's not responsive, don't pursue him further—and remember not to take his reaction personally. Don't let the little negative voices pull you down or tell you you're not good enough. Perhaps he has a girlfriend; perhaps you're not his type; never mind the reason, just move on. Never forget you are full of wonderful qualities that the right man will treasure.

Making Others Feel Comfortable

What kind of people make you feel comfortable? I always imagine a store clerk from a small-town store. When she or he is warm, friendly, and open, you feel comfortable immediately. If talking to a stranger is something totally foreign to you, and you feel like you're coming across in the wrong way, try this exercise actors use. Look in the mirror, pretend that you are looking at the guy, and say "Hello, my name is . . ." Do you sound warm and open? Stiff and uncomfortable? Do you look people in the eye when you say hello? Do you smile? It's amazing how few people make real eye contact or offer a genuine smile. Yet it can make all the difference in how people respond to you.

Make it your responsibility to put others at ease. At any social event, party or club, you'll find two types of people: the organizers, group leaders or hosts, and the followers or guests. Even at a bar, you can identify the leaders who are running around making sure everyone is comfortable, getting drinks and introducing people to one another. The followers are standing around waiting for someone to come and take care of them, to introduce them around. Try thinking like a leader at the next event you attend. If you're self-consciously thinking, "am I saying this right?" or "How am I coming across?" you'll be too distracted to give the person in front of you your full attention. Instead of obsessing over your own insecurities, how you look or feel, focus outward on how the other people in the room feel. Tell yourself for this one night it's your job to watch over the crowd, to take care of others. Be fully present with each new person you meet. For example, initiate a conversation with someone standing alone in a corner. Smile and introduce everyone you meet to one another.

You'll soon find that taking a leadership role will make you forget how uncomfortable you feel. Instead of being nervous, you'll begin to feel powerful. With only a little practice, your whole perspective will change. People will be drawn to you. Confidence comes from feeling you have control over your life, surroundings, and destiny. Your shyness will disappear and you'll hardly recognize the new you.

Other Confidence Tips

Being a good huntress is dependent on good self esteem. When you're empowered, you're courageous, daring and those you approach see you as dynamic. If you are really shy and nothing seems to work, try the following technique: Think of a famous actress you admire. Imagine she's not only beautiful, but confident, smart, and kind. The next time you leave your home and are walking down the street, imagine you're her. Obviously, she knows that people respect and admire her. Can you visualize yourself in her skin? She is not pretentious yet knows people are noticing her. How does she walk? With a little practice walking along the street as your favorite movie star, you'll see that people will start to treat *you* differently. It's amazing, but when you see yourself as popular and beautiful, you appear this way to others.

Confident women tend to have consistent personalities. Others, lacking confidence in meeting men or in new situations, have one personality at home with their family, another with their friends, another at the office, another on a date, and a completely different personality in public. Isolate and study these different sides of yourself. Where and with whom do you feel confident? Imagine you're talking to your two best friends or closest family members at your favorite place. Who are you at this moment? Study this person; she is the real you. The next time you have an insecurity attack draw on this strong, powerful, confident side of yourself. If you were with a friend who became incredibly nervous, insecure, or afraid, I'm sure you would put your arm around her and tell her she's safe. The trick is to summon the strong side of yourself to do this in new situations.

When you feel yourself spiraling downward into insecurity, practice accessing your strong, confident side, and demand that it rise up and fight for control. Conquering fear is a matter of understanding your mind and feelings and your own power over them. Don't let your insecurity spin out of control. With determination, you can control it. If there are people, places, and things that bring out the real you, seek them out. The more comfortable you are, the easier it will be for you to access your own inner strength.

Be Approachable

Leona, a gorgeous former model girlfriend of mine, is always complaining that she rarely gets asked out on dates. "How do you do it?" she asked. "You're always meeting men! No one asks me out or even looks at me." At a recent party, I had the opportunity to observe her while introducing her to some good-looking, eligible male friends. Although I knew her to be warm and friendly, her demeanor with strangers was just the opposite. Upon introducing herself, she stiffly stuck out her hand and said hello conservatively and cautiously. Within one second, she was looking over their shoulder for the next new face. She was afraid to look her new acquaintance in the eye and make a real connection. No wonder guys didn't want to talk to her! She came across as cold and aloof, which the men felt was a rejection of them. She might as well have been wearing a DO NOT DISTURB sign. The men thought she was snobby and rude when, in reality, she was just shy.

A top TV producer for fifteen years, Jeff is trained to observe. I asked him what else makes women unapproachable. "You mean like keeping a tunnel-vision conversation going with her girlfriends and pretending like men were never invented? Or acting like they're dating the guy they're talking with (even though he's a brother, office mate, gay, etc.)?"

How do you come across? Do you take the time, even if it's only for a minute, to focus on the person in front of you? Do you talk *with* people or *at* people? Everyone deserves respect and good manners, just as you do. "Nice to meet you" means nothing unless it's delivered warmly. For your actions to be in line with your words, smile, look the person in the eye, find a connection, and watch for feedback as you say, "It's very nice to meet you."

Make Opportunities

Meeting people is an opportunity not a chore. All too often we anticipate rejection and so never leave our group of friends. Venture out; be friendly. Even the most awkward situations can provide unexpected opportunities. Elevators, for instance, seem to be storerooms for stone faces. Everyone is always uptight. But I have developed a number of elevator comments that immediately get everyone smiling. Whenever I have the luck to be in an elevator full of men in the Wall Street area, I make a comment such as "Look at this; it's ten to one in here, and women complain there are no men left!" or "If my friends could see me now with eight good-looking men all to myself, they'd never believe it. I'm definitely coming downtown more often." The stiff shirts suddenly take their eyes off the ceiling, look at each other, and crack up. They suddenly become real people with personalities. It always amuses me and makes them laugh. It's much easier than you think to put people at ease. In my experience, most people welcome any excuse to drop their public facades.

You Snooze, You Lose

Don't wait to be approached by a great guy. It could take a week, a year, or your whole life. You must create the opportunity for him to get to know you. All it takes is having the courage for that first introduction. The story of my friend Lisa is a wonderful example of seizing the moment.

Lisa had seen Tim one evening at a bar with some friends. She suddenly realized he was leaving before she'd had time to meet him, so she literally stopped him at the door, took his coat off and insisted he stay "just a few minutes more." He resisted initially, saying he had to get up early for a skiing trip, but she was adamant. They hit it off and danced and talked all night. When he returned from his trip, Lisa bravely took the initiative again and invited him to a special movie premiere. Tim was very flattered by her attention and that first date led to many others. Within a year, Tim proposed to my bold friend, and they are now very happily married. He feels lucky to have such a strong, confident woman as his partner.

A Word About Social Drinking

My friend Ron swears that "for every two drinks a man consumes the girl becomes 20 percent better-looking, and men are willing to promise 20 percent more. If the guy has had more than five drinks, and it is after midnight, you shouldn't believe a word he says."

Although it's common to rely on alcohol to be more at ease and build confidence, you'll be wasting, not creating, opportunities. You can only make a first impression once. When your senses are dulled, you won't be sharp enough to pick up on the nuances of group or individual dynamics. If you love wine with dinner but know it goes straight to your head, order a wine spritzer instead. Try drinking a glass of milk to coat your stomach, or having a little snack before you leave the house.

Of course, it's common social practice for a man to offer to buy you a drink, but unless you're prepared to stick around for at least fifteen minutes, politely decline. You can buy your own drink or stick to water. There are other important reasons for this tactic:

- You won't feel obligated to continue the conversation until you finish "his" drink. Instead, you can end the conversation and move on at any time.
- A lot of guys have the ridiculous belief that a woman owes him something if he buys her a drink. Obviously, you don't owe anything except common courtesy, but the "no drink" policy avoids any misunderstanding.
- The chance for ulterior motives is now lessened. He knows you're interested in him, not in free drinks, and you know he's interested in knowing you, not in getting you drunk.

Remembering Names

Avoiding someone you know, just because you forgot their name, will make them feel much worse than, "I'm sorry, please remind me of your name," or "I'm having a mind blank. I forgot your name." Or clue in your hunting buddy. "I forgot the name of the guy wearing the red tie." She can stick her hand out as he approaches and say "Hi, I'm Sonya," then as soon as he says his name, you can say, "Sorry, Albert this is Sonya, Sonya this is Albert." Not only will it help you to remember but the recipient will feel closer to you. They feel gratitude that you're acknowledging and recognizing them. When you run into someone you don't know well, always start with your name, "Sue Loranger, I met you at Dakota's restaurant, nice to see you again."

My father, a politician, had his own special way to remember names. He suggested that when someone mentions their name, you should immediately think of a friend, family member, film star, or acquaintance you already know who has the same name. When you see them again, you'll easily remember they have the same name as so-and-so. Another technique is to use their name a few times in the conversation, to remember it through repetition.

Closing the Deal

Once you've started talking to a man, it won't take long to know from his body language and attitude whether or not he's interested. If he is, go ahead and move to the next phase: getting his telephone number or E-mail address. Remember, it's not about games, it's about communication. If your "click-quotient" is high it will be obvious to both of you. Remind yourself—you are not interested in men who aren't interested in you.

Whether you think he might be exactly your type, or just a fun date, when you part ways and he asks for your number, always make sure to get his as well. If you don't have business cards, get some made up with your name and phone number. Personal cards aren't tacky; they're neat and professional. And a lot smarter than the alternatives: having him walk away empty-handed, using a napkin, or scrambling to find a pen. Bring more than you think you'll need. It's better to have too many than to run short. But be selective; they're meant for new people you like and would be happy to hear from, not the general public. Never give your card out unless you already know you'd like to see him again.

If you have his phone number, then you can decide if you want to follow up or not. Without his number, you're at his mercy and schedule. So what do you say? When he asks for your phone number, give him your card and ask for his. If he doesn't have one, produce a pen and paper, which you've packed in advance. Once again, the simple direct method works best. "I've enjoyed talking to you, but it looks like we're leaving. Why don't we exchange numbers so we can continue this at another time." Or another great one is, "I'm planning to have a party in the next few weeks, and I'd love to invite you; do you have a card?" Then have a party! If a few of your girlfriends are on the same hunting program, you can organize a small dinner or party together and invite all these interesting new men.

If the guy has left or you didn't get the chance to exchange numbers, it's perfectly acceptable to give your card to one of his friends and say, "You know, I didn't get the chance to say good-bye, could you give your friend my card?" or "I didn't feel comfortable approaching him in a big group. Would you please give him my card and tell him I'd love to have a drink with him sometime?" Go for it; take the chance! Remember, some will call, some won't.

Flirting from afar worked well for me. One night, I kept catching the eye and smiling at a CB who was sitting at the next table with a large group. Before I left with my friends, I gave my card to one of his friends who was up getting drinks. Intrigued, the guy I liked called the next day. It turned out he was the social chairman for the Harvard Business School. On our dinner date we planned on getting all of my single girlfriends together for his next big event. The icing on the cake was that he sent me a copy of the Business School Prospectus with photos and information on 675 mostly single men. BINGO! How happy my girlfriends were with me! I made a list of all the single, interesting men I thought we'd like to meet, and he arranged a party! The odds were two to one, and one of my girlfriends met her future husband. Living courageously rewards you with outstanding results.

What If You Don't Want to Give out Your Number?

On the other hand, just because you talk to a guy doesn't mean you have to give him your phone number. If your intuition tells you otherwise, listen to it. If you're not very interested, don't give him your card. If you're not sure and might like more time to talk to him before a date, try saying "I'm difficult to reach, why don't you give me your number and I'll give you a call?" This puts you in the position of power. You can decide if you're going to call him and when. If you tell him you don't have a phone he'll know he's getting the big blow off. Try to be diplomatic. Here are some ideas: "My roommate works from home and I don't like to disturb her with personal calls, so it's easier for me to call you." Or you might decide to only give out your work number. Or make up a second card with a service number (at the cost of a few dollars a month, an answering service takes all calls for you). You've heard women say, "I don't know why I get mixed up with these crazy loser guys." Well, take responsibility—don't give them your phone number to begin with!

What Do You Do Now That You Have His Number?

Get the cards, take them home (the cards not the men), and make sure you put the phone numbers in an organized fashion in your "Cute Boy" phone book. Twelve pages stapled together labeled: Jan., Feb., March, etc., will do just fine. Include a note to remind you where you met and any specifics. Any information you've gathered about his hobbies or interests will come in handy later when you want to set up a date. You may think this is overkill, but it might be two to four weeks until you see him again. Don't think for a second that guys don't put little notes on your cards—they do! Remember, during the hunting phase, you should be meeting a lot of men. If you don't keep notes on who you meet, when he calls, you may confuse him with John, who you met at a party, or Mike, who you met in the park, and Dan may never call back again. This way, as soon as someone phones you, you can quickly grab your list and say, "Mark, yes, Mark" (and find Mark). You'll have enough vital information here to get the conversation off to a good start.

Exit Strategies

Some women avoid eye contact at all cost and will not engage in any conversations, because they are afraid of getting "stuck." Unless you're watching the room like a confident huntress, you'll be the hunted. "Horny Hank" will be history when you're aware of your surroundings. If you've walked the room and gone in for a closer look, you'll hopefully only start conversations with the men you're interested in. And if you are busy talking to the great CB of your choice, you won't have to worry about getting rid of unwanted suitors.

A friend of mine remarked, "Whether I'm looking for men or just hanging out with my girlfriends, I never know how to get rid of the men I'm not interested in. So I end up talking to no one." The answer? If you're not clicking, or you don't feel comfortable talking with somebody and want to get out of the conversation, then get out! Don't feel guilty. Who knows? He could be thinking the same thing and just staying with you because he doesn't want to be impolite or hurt your feelings. It's better to leave than waste both his and your time. So wipe any guilt right out of your mind and learn how to say good-bye. Easing out of a conversation quickly and politely is really very easy, yet for those who are not skilled, it can evoke great fear and awkwardness. Learn the art of the graceful exit.

Female Diplomacy 101

The wrong way: "I have to go to the bathroom," or "I'll be right back." Men have heard these 100 times. They are standard blow-off lines. You might as well say, "I'm through talking to you, bye!" If you're not coming back, give it closure. The right way: Start with a positive statement and then give him the zinger. Be very nice, positive, and friendly, look him right in the eye and say, "Listen, it was really nice talking to you, but I've got to dash now." As long as you sincerely include something along the lines of, "It was great talking to you," you can add almost anything you want. If he's been polite to you, he deserves courtesy in return. He'll understand that you have places to go and people to meet. If you are kind, polite, and honest, he's not going to take it badly.

What If He's Persistent?

He may try to convince you to stay, but just be firm and say it again. When a business meeting is over, you shake hands, say good-bye, and no one feels hurt or upset. It's all in the delivery. When you say good-bye, whenever possible, use his name. It helps him feel you really acknowledged him and leaves him with a good feeling. That's the mission here, right? Remember, confidence and kindness. Need more examples?

- "I've taken up a lot of your time, Stan, I'm sure there are a lot of other girls here who want to meet a great guy like you."
- "Listen, Paul, I can see my girlfriend is getting a bit antsy. She and I rarely get together, and I need to spend some time with her. We're going to go mingle, but I've really enjoyed talking to you."
- "I see one of my friends from college across the room— if you'll excuse me, Max, I'm going to go over and say hello. It was a pleasure meeting you."
- "We're on our way out, but I'd like to thank you very much for the conversation."
- Look at your watch and say, "Wow, my friends have been waiting for me for twenty minutes. Time flies when

you're having fun." Give him a wink, shake his hand, and you're off.

- "It's been very nice talking to you, Mike, but I've been neglecting my friends. If you'll excuse me, I'm going to catch up with them."

- "Listen Jeff, I'm usually quite successful at setting my friends up and I think you might like my friend Linda, I know she'd like you. If you let me know how I can reach you I'll suggest she calls you or I'll call you with her number."

Be as sincere as possible. People respect and respond to kindness. "I've been locked up working for the last three weeks, and this is my first night out, I'm getting antsy, so I'm going to go walk around. I really enjoyed talking to you; you're a really great guy." When you leave, he'll be thinking, "She was nice." You won't hurt anyone's feelings if you abide by this exit strategy. Keep in mind, the guys who use the shotgun theory (if they hit on tons of women, one will eventually say yes) are used to being shot down. Your genuineness will be a breath of fresh air. If you pass him again during the night, don't avoid him. Look him right in the eye, give a wave or a smile as you pass, ask him how he's doing or say, "We meet again." Don't make him or yourself uncomfortable by trying to hide.

It's equally important to know when someone is cueing you that they'd like to leave. Be graceful. Usually it's nothing personal; some people have short attention spans. Others are out with friends they haven't seen in a long time. Others don't want to lose their ride home. If you feel it's none of the above and you're just not his type, think of it this way: at least he's giving you an honest signal not to waste your time. There are lots more CBs out there who *do* want to get to know you.

Remember

- Don't invade his space by standing too close.
- Put others at ease by showing genuine interest and concern.
- Get cards made and take them with you.
- Always carry a pen.
- If you like him, always get his number when you give him yours.

8

· · · · · · · · · · · · · · · · · · · ·

Setting Up the Date

· · · · · · · · · · · · · · · · · · · ·

As she noticed Anna sitting on the step, Katie rested for a moment, breathing deeply and sipping from her water bottle. Skating over to Anna's was a great workout.

"Guess what?" Anna called out. "John said he would love to go out with me!"

"You mean John the CB we beat at pool? You called him?"

As she laced up her rollerblades Anna replied, "Why wait for the weather report when you can create your own storm?"

For those of you who have been brainwashed that a woman never calls a man, take a breath and prepare yourself. The old, passive dating traditions don't make sense anymore. How great would it be if you could decide when your date would be, where you would go, and what you would do? It's a privilege men have had for years. Now you can have it, too. Once you conquer your fear, it's unbelievably easy. Change your mind-set. Change your prejudices. And change your behavior. You can have as many dates as you wish—it's (literally) your call! It's not what you do that hurts your chances, it's what you don't do.

Let's face it: even if we can forget what we've been taught, most of us are too reserved or afraid of rejection to call a man. Instead, we sit back and wonder why men aren't calling us. Even strong, successful career women seldom take matters into their own hands by arranging their dates. Men have the same fears yet overcome them on a regular basis, acknowledged Roger, a thirty-three-year-old electrical engineer, "For every one girl I call, there are nine more I psych myself out of calling."

Kent, a thirty-year-old financial reporter, agrees. "I'm fed up with always having to make the first move. I want a straightforward woman, one who knows she's interested in me. Any guy would be flattered if a woman takes the pressure off and makes the first call." If you're happy and confident with your life, it will feel like the most natural thing in the world to both of you.

Empower yourself through practice. When setting up a date, the same three steps from "The Approach" apply: (1) pick the right time; (2) always introduce yourself; and (3) let the conversation flow comfortably. Only by talking to the opposite sex will you overcome your fears and discover you have something to say. It's your choice: stay afraid, passive, and alone, or be proactive and create a life full of dates, new friends, and good times.

How to Get Started

By now, after following the advice in the first few chapters, you have organized your "CB Book" and entered a few numbers. A week and a half has slipped by, they haven't called you, and you'd like to set up some dates. Remember, you wouldn't have asked for their numbers unless you felt a connection. So what do you do?

Simple. Call and ask them if they'd like to get together. Yes! Gasp! I know, suddenly you'd rather climb Mt. Everest or even clean out your refrigerator. But I promise, after the first few times, your confidence will grow, and you'll kick yourself for not taking control sooner. Remember, nothing ventured, nothing gained!

Don't Take Rejection Personally

One of the biggest mistakes women make is to attribute a man's behavior to themselves. Never assume a man's actions are because of you. This is the major reason women derail their dating self-confidence. If a man doesn't call, nine out of ten women view this as a commentary on their personal attractiveness. They assume they've been rejected, that they're not good enough. A man may not call for a million different reasons. It's wrong to assume that it's a negative reflection on you! My friend Brad, who wrote a book on what men want, says that men call only 20 percent of the women they like whose numbers they've asked for.

Too often women get depressed and feel responsible. Don't work yourself up trying to imagine why he hasn't called. The only way you'll know is to ask an honest mutual friend. He could think you're the world's greatest girl, but there could also be a million reasons your phone isn't ringing, most of which have nothing to do with you. Don't waste time worrying and don't let his failure to make the first move slow you down or create self-doubts. He's human, just like you. He may not have called because:

- he's afraid of rejection.
- he was busy and is afraid he waited too long.
- he's shy.
- he's been consumed by a recent project at work.
- nothing is working in his life right now and all his energy is going into survival.
- your phone number went into the wash with his jeans.
- he'd had a few drinks and came home with three or four phone numbers.

Under these circumstances, a call from you could easily start the ball rolling. Your call will be appreciated. On the other hand, his reasons for not calling may run more along the lines of:

- his old girlfriend showed up the day after he met you.
- he already has a girlfriend.
- he's gay.
- he's dating several girls already and doesn't want to complicate his life with additional relationships.
- he needs more time to get over his ex.
- he may sense you want a relationship, and he's a chronic bachelor.

Under these circumstances, your call may or may not generate a date. However, remember in no way is this a rejection of you personally. Honestly, what do any of these reasons have to do with you? Nothing. So just dust yourself off and move on.

Men deal with the fear of rejection all the time. If you want amazing results, you'll have to learn to deal with it just like they do. This means not taking every "no" personally. Men call it "playing the odds." They call five girls and get dates with two. Why can't you do the same? Even in a sales presentation, five people might say no to your product, but one is going to say yes. And that's all you need. Luckily, most will say yes. So take the plunge. Be brave. It's what will set you apart from other women—and the right man will appreciate that.

Making the Call

A week after you've met an interesting guy is the right time to call—not before. There's a difference between taking control and being overaggressive. Everyone is busy with their lives; give *him* a chance to act. The exception to this is E-mail. If you have his E-mail address (happily supplied by his card, secretary, or office) go ahead and send a note telling him that you enjoyed meeting him. "Hi John, great meeting you at Pete's the other night, I really enjoyed our conversation. And by the way, I was serious about my offer to help you with introductions in the publishing world if you'd like. Look forward to staying in touch. Kelsey." The great thing about E-mail is that it's non-threatening and he can read it at his leisure.

When you make contact by phone or E-mail, the first thing you need to do is to reintroduce yourself. No matter how sure you are that he'll remember you, always give him a little reminder of who you are. Describe yourself quickly and distinctly. Don't expect him to remember you without a description—any intriguing, socially active man will be meeting several women a week. Be confident and friendly. Let him know you thought he was an interesting person and that you'd like to get together. For example: "Hi, this is Sonya. I met you in the park with my son." "Hi, this is Marnie. I'm the film producer. We met at Jim McMullen's party."

After you have reintroduced yourself, get to the point of your call. You should have already made some decisions regarding the type of date you're after. Do you want to make a one-on-one lunch or dinner date, ask him to a special event, or take the pressure off and invite him to a party or to join a group of friends? You need to decide what will make both of you feel most comfortable. For example: "This is Camilla. I met you at the health food restaurant. I know a few other interesting health food restaurants, and I thought I'd call and see if you'd like to try one. Would you have any interest in joining me?"

Keep in mind that it's important to propose open-ended choices. For example, you might say: "There are some great movies out right now," and then give him options—action adventure or comedy. And give him a choice on days—"I'm free Monday, Friday, or Sunday night." By offering options, you're getting his input and you're more likely to be successful.

Think back to when you met him. What did you learn about his interests? "I remember you like the Knicks. There's a game on Thursday. I have a friend who can get me tickets, and I wondered if you'd like to join me." (There is something innocent and nonthreatening about an afternoon date: a baseball game, roller-skating in the park, going to a street fair.) On the other hand, don't sacrifice yourself. If you hate baseball, don't pretend you love it. Instead, pick something that interests both of you.

A friend of mine, Enid, found out Kevin liked music; she called and invited him to hear her sing at a club. For date number two, she invited him to a show starring her cousin; and then called again to invite him to the Thanksgiving Day parade. Kevin was focused on his career, so it took several occasions before he realized this relationship was enriching his life. A couple of months later, they were discussing marriage and have now been happily married for five years and have a beautiful baby girl.

If you don't know of any common interests, ask him to get his calendar out. "I'm sure your book is pretty full, but I hope you can pen me in for a drink." Men love to have their egos boosted, and he'll probably find your comment sassy and flirtatious and get a kick out of it. Or just keep it simple. "I enjoyed meeting you, and I thought it would be fun to get together again. What's your schedule like? What day would be good for you?" Or, "I had fun talking to you last week. I wanted to say hi and touch base." Or even, to test the waters, "I have a really busy week ahead, and things are crazy at work, but when things calm down, it would be great to meet for a drink."

If some time has gone by or if you still feel intimidated calling him, you can try some creative approaches. You might say, "Hi, Jack. This is Andrea, the actress from Florida. I was organizing my desk at work and found your card and thought I'd call." or, "I'm sorry I didn't call you sooner but my schedule has been so hectic. Things are finally slowing down." (Most guys will be flattered that you thought of them again.) Go with whatever feels comfortable. Be natural and confident. Remember, you're only suggesting a date!

Phone Manners

Many men have told me, "If a girl seems uninterested after one or two calls, I'll drop her." Give him positive feedback. If you're interested, don't act coy. Let him into your world. Tell him about your interests and ambitions. Across the board, men I spoke with agreed, "If a woman does not call me back after a few times, I'll stop calling." So ignore advice that suggests you do otherwise. Women who don't return phone calls are rude. Don't get caught up in these games. A man will think, "It's impolite. I wasn't brought up that way, and I wouldn't want to date someone who was." If you like him but will be busy at the time he suggests, he may feel embarrassed or think you aren't really interested. It may deter him from calling again. So don't forget to tell him you'd love to get together another time, and set it up while you have him on the phone.

Accepting "No" Gracefully

If someone sends signals that he's not interested, cut your losses. And again, don't take it personally. Above all, accept his message with grace. Don't pester him or ask him why he's not interested. Think how uncomfortable it would make you feel if a guy kept pushing you like that. If he's not interested, let it go. At that point, you can't make it better. Why would you want someone who doesn't want you?

Keep your efforts to three calls. If he hedges or doesn't call back after the third, he's toast! If he's inconsiderate, rude, or loaded down with emotional baggage, you don't want him anyway. End of story. Three strikes and he's out.

Eight Phone Tips

First, choose your timing carefully, taking into account any little details you know about his lifestyle. If you call someone at the wrong time, a negative association may arise. The goal is to try and catch him at a relaxed moment. If you do reach him, and he seems unreceptive, remember it probably has nothing to do with you. He could simply be having a bad day. If he's at the office and sounds hurried, he may have an urgent meeting or deadline. Open with: "I know you're busy at the office. Is this a good time?" If not, he'll tell you. Ask when it would be better to try again. Don't act offended—you shouldn't be. He has other things going on in his life, just as you do.

If you're setting up a date for the following week, the best time to phone him at the office is on Thursday or Friday between 4:00 and 6:00 P.M. Afternoons at the end of the week are often slower and quieter, and he's more likely to have time to talk. Psychologically, he'll be starting to unwind. With his work essentially done, how can he resist a call from an interesting woman? He should feel comfortable making plans for the following week unless he proposes the weekend and you're free.

If you prefer to call him at home, try between 6:30 and 7:30 P.M. By then, most people are home from work, have had a few moments to relax, and aren't yet on their way out again.

Second, when you call, if you get a machine, a roommate, a receptionist, a secretary—anything of this sort—be polite but don't leave a message. If they ask you who's calling so they can leave him a message, just say, "I'll try again later; when do you expect him back?" The key is to reach him in person. This keeps the ball in your court. In person you can remind him who you are, make a positive impression, and, most important, get him to start flipping through his calendar.

Third, once you get a chance to talk, you'll quickly get a sense of whether or not you're clicking with him. If you're initiating the call, you'll learn to sense in the first few minutes whether he is enjoying the conversation. And it should only take a few seconds to figure out if it's a good time to talk. (If not, try: "You sound preoccupied; would you like me to call you later?")

Fourth, if you're relaxed and happy when you speak, it will put him at ease. This means taking an interest in him. For instance, if you sense he has time to talk, ask him what he likes to spend his time doing and really listen to the answer. Everyone likes to feel special. And don't be afraid to use humor; a little joking takes the pressure off everyone. Make him smile. And if you feel like the conversation is starting to stretch, or you're finding it difficult to talk, it's much better to finish quickly and leave a short, favorable impression than to drag it out.

Fifth, on the other hand, if you suddenly find yourself engrossed in a conversation, go with the flow. Remember, great bonds and great relationships spring from great communication. Don't play hard to get. Why should you cut short a fascinating, engaging talk with a wonderful man by playing hard to get and ending the call? He'll be insulted. You'll send the message, "I'm sorry, but I don't have time to get to know you."

Sixth, don't play silly phone games. Women sometimes resort to these things—calls at 2:00 A.M. to see if he's home, calls after you've had too much to drink. Nothing will present you in a more negative light. This merely shows a man that you use very poor judgment or have no life.

Seventh, don't call every ten minutes to catch him in person. He may have Caller I.D. and will be turned off by your overeagerness. Besides, he should not be your main event. You and your goals should be. You don't want to come across as a girl who's desperate for a relationship. No one wants to feel threatened by having their personal space invaded.

Last of all, when you ask him out, don't overanalyze what he says; guys usually mean what they say. Don't script your conversations. Keep it light. And finish your conversation with something upbeat. Instead of saying, "Talk to you later," try, "It was great talking to you; I hope you have a good week [or weekend]."

Creative Date Planning

When planning a date, instead of the standard, "Let's have dinner or drinks," try something different. Think lively and active, not romantic—you'll have lots of time for that after you get to know him! You might pick a Japanese restaurant where you sit on the floor or a Greek restaurant where you can break the plates. Shoot a game of pool. Take a helicopter ride. Go to a concert in the park. Scout out places for picnics. How about an art gallery opening? Or suggest something really unique, like going to your local health club and trying the new mountain climbing wall. Often, the most creative dates involve an activity such as horseback riding, running, mountain biking, or Rollerblading.

If you're going away for the day, make sure there will be recreational activities available such as golf, skiing, a museum, the beach, a fair, or an amusement park. Get ideas from local magazines, books, or your Sunday paper for offbeat places in your city. Even if you're on the "standard" date, do something spontaneous, exciting, and fun. It could be as simple as stopping to buy him a Pez candy dispenser or going to a cigar bar, buying him a cigar and popping it into his mouth. When my girlfriend Bridget found out her date also loved photography, she suggested photographing interesting things around the city. What could have been an average date turned into a creative romp through the urban jungle.

If you want to remove any pressure, invite him as a new friend to join you and a small group of friends for a movie or a drink at your favorite watering hole. Here are a few examples of creative, successful first date-strategies.

My friend Donna was sure Scott liked her. But she was painfully shy and afraid to ask him out. She and I had movie plans one weekend. I suggested she tell him "a friend and I are getting together, and we would love you to join us." He accepted her offer. I then suggested she ditch me right after the movie. I explained, "Sorry to dash—I have to get home to work on my book." Now married to Scott, Donna always jokes that I went on their first date.

Alex, a good-looking, popular band leader, has a great story of a no-pressure invitation. "I met a woman at a party. She called and said she was getting together with a group of good friends—male and female—for a picnic in Central Park. She said they would enjoy meeting me. It sounded nonthreatening.

It wasn't going to be just the two of us. I thought it sounded intriguing. When I got there, I sat next to her, and found out how compatible we were. We ended up dating."

Here's Tim's story. "Candice called me up with two tickets to the U.S. Open. Later, she told me she'd played tennis for the University of Pennsylvania. I found that really interesting. That first date was the start of a very beautiful relationship. I think it's awesome that she called me, and it was an amazing date."

If someone at work comes by on a Friday and says, "Hey, I've got two great theater or sports tickets, do you want them?" start thinking who you want to invite. Your girlfriends? No. You'll see them later in the week. Get on the phone and go down your CB list.

Spontaneity

Most men and women have a lot going on in their lives, and almost everyone feels pressure, whether it's to move ahead in their careers, keep fit, or stay in touch with friends and family. Many people often put in exhausting hours to succeed and move up the corporate ladder. Their work can totally consume them. Only later in the work week do real achievers slow down and plan their weekend. Therefore, a man can still be sincere if he calls and, giving you short notice, asks you out on Thursday or Friday for a Saturday date.

Men tire quickly of high-maintenance women who need to be penciled in days in advance. These women ruin the thrill of occasional last-minute tickets or spur-of-the-moment planning. They irritate rather than attract. Accept any date with a man you like, even if he springs it on you at the last minute. If you want to go out, then go. Spontaneity can be very attractive. It's part of your strength. And you'll be doing something interesting and fun on a Saturday night, instead of punishing both yourself and him because he didn't call early enough.

Don't pretend you have something to do when you really

want to be with him. Otherwise, he'll take the time he wanted to spend with you getting to know someone else. Time is a valuable commodity, so don't waste a great offer or a Saturday night by staying home to watch television just to prove you're hard to get. Get out there! When you sit at home and wallow in loneliness, your self-esteem plummets and you're less likely to attract the right people. On the other hand, it's important never to do anything because you're desperate. Staying at home and working on a project that interests you is never a bad alternative. Don't play games and tell him you have plans if you've simply decided to stay in on a Saturday night. Be honest and say, "I'm staying home to get some work done." He's not going to think you're a loser, he'll be impressed that you have interests and ambitions.

Most importantly, don't listen to that little voice saying, "I can't call a man." You can and you will. Be bold! It's the new you! It's time to take matters into your own hands. I know you can do it. Riding a bike was scary the first time. So was the first day of school. With a change in attitude, this will become an exciting adventure. Yes, you're taking a risk and yes, there will be times when the man you call is busy or unresponsive. That's why you're keeping several irons in the fire.

Remember

- Don't take it personally if he doesn't call you.
- Take back your own power and make that first call.
- Introduce yourself and remind him who you are.
- Don't leave a message. Wait for the best time to speak to him in person.
- Don't play games. If he calls you, call him back. If you want to see him, set up the earliest mutually convenient time.
- Be creative and spontaneous in planning your dates or accepting his offers.

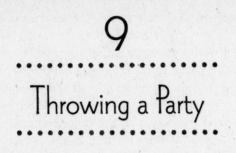

9

Throwing a Party

As Katie sipped her cranberry seltzer and surveyed the guest list, she could feel her excitement mounting.

"Louise will be so happy and surprised that we didn't forget to throw her birthday party this year."

Anna flashed a smile and nodded. Katie knew that look of Anna's.

"Anna, what aren't you telling me?"

With a big grin, Anna shared her secret: "Well, since you must know, I took the liberty of inviting all the CB's we've met recently."

Still too nervous to ask someone out on a date? Then throw a party. The atmosphere is relaxed, the pressure is off, and you can shape the evening however you'd like. Moreover, as the hostess, you'll be making a difference by introducing interesting people to one another.

For most people, time and cost are the biggest deterrents to having a party. Think of creative solutions to overcome this. Can you throw the party with a friend? That will cut both in half. If you don't know many people, organize a party with a group of friends where each one brings their nicest male friend. Let the sparks fly. Perhaps one of your friends has a bigger apartment and you can have the party there. Promise to take care of the cleanup—and keep your word. For something inexpensive and different, organize a large picnic in the park. Suggest hats and sun dresses as the dress code (don't forget to schedule a rain date). Specify exactly where in the park and bring blankets. Or brunch followed by ice or roller-skating.

Parties don't have to cost a lot. Most of what you'll need can be bought very reasonably and in bulk. Look under party supplies in your local phone book. There are wholesale companies that deliver large buckets of ice, tables, linens, glasses, and even coat racks. If you're on a very tight budget, having a small group over to watch the presidential debates, Academy Awards, tennis tournament, or a new movie and ordering pizza is better than sitting at home bored and lonely. In fact, the most casual situations often make people feel most at ease.

Preparing for the Party

It's not difficult to throw a party, but for things to run smoothly you need to be organized. Pick a date about three weeks in the future. Round up one or two reliable friends to help you. Then start planning.

The Guest List

Before inviting the masses, call your best friends to coordinate a date that works with them. Then include as many interesting and fun people as the room will comfortably hold. But don't invite people just to fill a room. Weed out acquaintances you think might pull the party down and make your other guests uncomfortable. If you fear a large party might get out of control, hire a bouncer to stand at the entrance with a guest list (if you're on a budget ask a good male friend to stand in for an hour or two). Letting all invited guests know in advance that this is by invitation only or that you will have a guest list at the door will help intimidate crashers. Keep in mind that approximately 20 percent of the people who say they'll be there won't show up due to numerous reasons (dinner was extended, they were too tired, unexpected other events, etc.).

Invitations

It's always a nice touch to send invitations. And you can have fun creating them. For one Valentine's party I used a photo of my best friends and me in red dresses. Another time I made a collage of all group party shots on one side of the card, had it photocopied and printed the invitation on the back. For a friend's surprise birthday party I got a cute baby photo from her mom. You can buy patterned preprinted packs from the store or, if you're handy with a computer, you can buy patterned paper and customize them yourself. Try scanning in any photo or even a collage. Some stores, like Hallmark, offer several selections and do the work for you.

For formal invitations or larger parties you might want to research professional printers in the Yellow Pages. It's really not that expensive, and worth the cost if you're going all-out. For a large party it can be much more efficient to simply E-mail the invitation to everyone with the click of a key! But if you do use E-mail, add a personal note letting them know how much you hope they can make it. And give a call a week before the event to any CBs and important friends to make sure they got the invite and to tell them you're anticipating a great, fun crowd.

Guests should be invited by phone, E-mail or snail mail between three weeks to ten days before the event. By giving them ample notice, you build anticipation and make them aware of the effort you're putting into the event. Invitations should include time, location or address, dress code, and names of all of the hosts/hostesses. Make things easy by having "Regrets Only" as an RSVP and include a phone number with an answering machine to collect messages. While doing your head count, know that a number of people will forget to RSVP even if they can't come. Have your guest list near the phone to help you keep track of who calls.

Location

Pick a good environment, one where you feel comfortable. Examples might include your apartment, a friend's apartment, or a private room in a restaurant. If you're bringing in a large group, you'll be surprised at the great deals you can arrange with a local restaurant, hotel, or bar with a little negotiating. Offer to have your event on an off night or after regular hours. Many apartment buildings and community centers have party rooms they rent out very affordably.

Wherever you decide to have the party, make sure it's clean, that there's plenty of space and handy bathroom facilities. If the party is in your apartment, for example, move furniture into another room or off to the side. People congregate near the food and drinks, so put them in the largest room. Put coats on the bed or arrange to rent a coat rack.

Mood

Buy low-wattage bulbs or turn the lights down. Light-pink- and peach-colored bulbs are the most flattering. Candles add a nice touch—but be careful, you don't want your mood lighting to scorch the ceiling or set the drapes on fire. My friend Zackie always attends to every little detail at her dinner parties. One year she set up a Thanksgiving Day feast with all sorts of ornaments. A few minutes after we sat down to dinner I smelled smoke. When I stuck my head into the living room there was a blaze hitting the roof! The slightly opened window had blown the candle into the large dried-flower arrangement. It was quite a funny sight as the whole group was running around with soaked towels. Tips for avoiding this scene: If you float votive candles in a glass with a little water, they last longer and can't tip over.

Flowers and Plants

Another nice touch, flowers can set the mood for different corners of the room, lighting them up or hiding overflowing belongings. Your guests may think to bring them, so borrow vases if you need to. Put them where everyone can see them— but where they won't get knocked over. Keep them away from the stereo!

Music

Good music is key. First, decide what type of mood you want. Is your party a wine-and-cheese affair that cries out for classical music? Or will people be dancing? Plan the music accordingly. Ask your friends for their selections. If you know someone who's a deejay or who works at a bar or dance club, ask what kind of music works best. Ask friends for copies of their party tapes. Don't use the radio—no one wants to listen to commercials at a party.

Assign a reliable friend to supervise the music. Try starting with something slow and calming . . . and then speed things up later. Make sure everyone can talk easily over the music. If you're planning on dancing, try to keep the dance floor near the stereo, so that those not dancing can still hear each other. A cloth over the stereo equipment will help soak up a possible overturned drink.

Alcohol

Vodka, gin, rum, and scotch are the four most requested "hard" alcohols. Vodka usually goes the fastest, so have plenty on hand (you can always save it for the next party). If margaritas are on the menu, you'll need tequila. Include a selection of beer and wine (red and white), and soft drinks (regular and diet), or seltzer and juices (orange and cranberry) for the teetotalers and designated drivers. If your event is outdoors, a keg can cut down on beer costs.

As for punches, try mixing ½ gallon orange juice (with pulp), ½ gallon tropical fruit mix (banana, pineapple, etc.), ½ gallon cranberry juice, and a two-liter bottle of ginger ale. Mix it all in a large punchbowl. (Borrow one if necessary and consider investing in one for the future.) This mix, without alcohol, can be premade in pitchers and kept cold in the refrigerator. Any combination of vodka, rum, peach schnapps, or apricot brandy will add a kick to it—but let people know if the punch is alcoholic. Many a guest has downed glass after glass only to find they've been talking to the lampshade all night! Also, for those who are driving, it is important they know what they're drinking. Remember, one tequila, two tequila, three tequila, floor!

Party Snacks

The easiest thing to do is to schedule the party after everyone has already eaten. That way you're limited to traditional snacks (pretzels, chips, Doritos, crackers, cheese, candy, or desserts). If you have things that can be eaten in one bite without a plate, then cleanup is a snap.

Additional Drink Tips

For groups larger than forty to fifty people, keep two or three extra cans of frozen orange juice in the freezer, just in case. Before your guests arrive, prepare lemons, limes, cherries, cut pineapple, and other "extras" for drinks. For summer exotica, try colored straws and tiny umbrellas with a piece of fruit. For larger groups, I've found the large, clear plastic glasses, to be best. You can see what's in them and when filled they are heavier and thus less likely to spill. When preparing drinks, fill the glasses up with ice—you'll have many less half-full drinks left on the tables. Also, don't forget to have a blender on hand if you're planning to serve margaritas or piña coladas. Finally, make sure to put drink coasters and ashtrays all over the house. You don't want your furniture stained by absentminded guests.

Hired Help

If you are expecting more than thirty people the cost of a "helper" is worth every penny. For six to fifteen dollars an hour, you can have a college student or a professional cleaning person on hand to help answer the door, pour drinks, take coats, cut limes and lemons, collect empty glasses, and clean up during the party. Ask them to wear a white shirt and black skirt or pants—they'll look more professional and be differentiated from the guests. It can make a huge difference. You'll enjoy yourself a lot more and you won't have a big mess at the end of the evening.

Being a Good Hostess

A good hostess is more concerned about her guests than herself, and watches the crowd to make sure everyone is having a good time. Every twenty minutes or so, mix up the little groups that have formed by introducing them to the newcomers. I often ask my best friend to help: "Sonya I'd like you to meet Amanda; she just moved here from Canada and doesn't know anyone. Would you mind taking her around and introducing her to everyone for me?" Split up people who know each other well by mixing them with other people if you think they'll click. Obviously, if two people are involved in a deep conversation, leave them alone.

It's your job as hostess to introduce people to one another. A good introduction includes the person's name and some details about them. "Josh is a fantastic piano player." "Pam is a masseuse." "This is Matt. He's an accountant and loves Ireland." Or, "Let me introduce you to Ron. He's the funniest guy you'll ever meet. He's from Toronto, and he's a great skier." Having a little information about each other helps people feel comfortable, and it immediately gives them something to talk about. It also gives them the freedom to approach the person later, if they want to.

Getting nervous about the party won't change the outcome.

Alert your neighbors in advance and ask for their tolerance. Stay calm, cool, and collected, yet be prepared for Murphy's Law (If anything can go wrong it will!) to kick in at anytime. Plan everything to be ready at least two hours before the doorbell rings; this way you can take a leisurely shower, put on some great music and take your time getting ready. When guests arrive you'll be calm, fully present, and gracious.

Finally, it's vital to make sure no one drives home drunk. If someone has had too much to drink, confiscate their keys and either ask another friend to drive them to their destination or call a taxi.

Shopping List

(This list can accommodate up to 100 people. Divide the amounts in half for 50 or less.)

3 lemons, 3 limes
2 64-fl-ounce bottles of cranberry juice
3 two-liter bottles of Diet Coke
3 two-liter bottles of soda water
2 one-liter bottles of tonic water
2 half-gallon cartons of orange juice with pulp
2 half-gallon cartons of orange juice/exotic blend, e.g., pineapple/peach/mango
2 two-liter bottles of diet 7UP
2 two-liter bottles of ginger ale
5 bags of ice, crushed if possible
300 clear plastic glasses (always buy three times what you think you'll need)
3 large cans of frozen orange juice (for the freezer)
Large garbage bags
Toilet paper
Paper towels
Ziploc or other resealable freezer bags
3 large bunches of red seedless grapes
2 large bunches of green seedless grapes
1 large wheel of brie

Boxes of crackers
Large popcorn/chips or other munchies
3 cases of beer
Wine: 6 bottles of white, 3 of red (your guests will arrive
    with more)
2 gallons of vodka
1 gallon of rum
1 liter of scotch (for a mature crowd also add 1 liter of
    bourbon)
1 liter of gin

The Small Dinner Party

One of the best social invitations is a small dinner. Eight
to sixteen people is a great number, big enough to create excitement and diversity, but still small enough for great conversation and really getting to know one another. Consider
organizing a small dinner at a restaurant. Do some research:
Find one that's reasonable and has great atmosphere, prefera-
bly with a bar where everyone can meet and mingle before-
hand. Approach the owner and say you'd like to organize a
dinner or party for a group of ten or more people. Most will be
happy to have your business. They will often even throw in a
few bottles of wine on the house. Don't forget to ask about special discounts or menus; prix fixe menus are usually much
cheaper. Or ask them to print up a special menu minus any of
their really expensive items. This ensures that everyone has a
great meal at an affordable price. Mention in advance that you
plan to split the bill equally among all your guests. Cards like
IGT, Transmedia, and Diners Club take 10 to 20 percent off the
bill at designated restaurants, so don't forget to ask in advance
if any discounts are possible.

Ask people to come for 7:30 or 8:00 P.M., and plan to sit
down around 9:00. Arrive on time with a seating plan and
place name cards around the table, based on those you think
would enjoy speaking to each other. Seat yourself last.

When you're the hostess of a dinner at a restaurant, it's your responsibility to preorder the wine. Pick something decent and reasonable. If you let the wrong person take over this job, everyone's bill will be doubled. It's also your duty to get the bill sorted out fairly; for example, if Dave ordered a steak and Mary only had a side salad, a small whisper in Dave's ear for ten dollars extra will ensure Mary doesn't leave upset. If necessary, excuse yourself first and go to the waiters' station to look at the bill. Be clear on exactly who ate a meal and who didn't. Ask the waiter to do the math on a calculator. Don't forget to include a tip. One very successful method I use is to have the men pay 10 to 20 percent more than the women. Why? Men usually have bigger appetites and often drink more. I find the men don't mind making a slightly larger contribution when they've ordered more.

If you're having dinner at home and don't want a messy cleanup, try the heavy black plastic cutlery available at most party stores. There are also quite nice heavy plastic plates. Watch out for thin paper ones that leak and bend under the weight of the food. Casseroles prepared ahead of time are inexpensive and easy. I find it's easier to have the food set up as a buffet than to try to pass dishes around the table. Make sure to have a box of large freezer bags on hand so leftovers can be stored and frozen. A well-planned dinner should be easy for you and a lot of fun for everyone else. Pat yourself on the back; you have initiated and created an enjoyable experience for all.

Some Final Party Tips

Party Favors Buy some cute little toys or fun games and put one at each seat. At my birthday party each year, I take a group shot and everyone who attended last year gets a framed enlargement waiting on their chair. Want some other ideas? An envelope with copies of the photos from your last party (everyone likes to pass photos around), party crackers, fortune cookies with your own message, festive masks. It will bring back great memories and provide them with an easy conversation starter. Buy a few disposable cameras with flashes and leave them on the tables.

Games   Give everyone a card with the names of three people you want them to meet that night. This works especially well when people don't know each other. They'll soon discover why you chose those particular people for them to meet.

Musical Chairs   Try having each man move two seats to the left at dessert. One time I did this at dinner, and it turned out two shy friends ended up exactly where they had wished to be to begin with: the start of a very serious relationship.

Make a Short Speech   Thank your guests for coming and point out any exciting trivia. For example, congratulate Joanie on her upcoming birthday, Steve on his new job, your best friends for being their wonderful selves. Everyone is interested in discovering who the other people at the table are, how you know them, and why you love them. This will help bond your friends, new and old.

Be Courteous   Alert your neighbors in advance and ask for their tolerance.

Being a Good Guest

When you attend a party, help your hostess by introducing yourself to anyone you don't already know, and make an effort to include them in your conversations. If someone looks left out, strike up a conversation. Be inclusive, not exclusive.

And please: Never, ever, switch name cards at a seated dinner. The host knows all the guests and has the best idea how to make everyone happy.

Remember

- Think of creative solutions to overcome cost and time restraints.
- Don't hesitate to assign tasks to trustworthy friends.
- The responsibilities of the hostess include making introductions and making sure all the guests meet, mingle, and enjoy themselves.
- Ensure the restaurant bill is fairly distributed.

PART III

Dating

10
. . . .
The First Few Dates
. . . .

Katie licked her lips as she and Louise looked at the spread Anna had cooked up. "My favorite, extra cheese lasagna!"

"Do I know you or what?" Anna replied. "Now dig in and tell me about your date last night."

Katie gulped. "Yikes, let's not go through that again. He spent the whole evening flirting with the Czechoslovakian waitress."

"I can top that," Louise chirped in. "Once I had a blind date who drove me across town to use his two-for-one coupon at a dive restaurant and when we got there it had expired!" Katie reflected as she continued. "Well, all was not lost. We bumped into a CB he works with and when my date from hell was paying the bill and getting the waitress's phone number, I exchanged cards with his coworker!"

The first few dates can be nerve-wracking—some are even downright unbearable. But as you start to screen and choose who you want to go out with (instead of dating the men who call you) you'll find your dates are a lot more interesting and fun.

Preparing for the Date

Since I am a fashion designer, everyone always calls me to ask what to wear on a hot date. My answer is always the same.

Go to your closet and flip through your hangers. Stop at the items you feel most confident and comfortable in. Dress for your mood on that particular evening. Avoid wearing anything too tight, extravagant, or "statement-making." If you look soft and feminine it can also help you feel that way. Confidence and femininity is an intoxicating mixture. The more natural and comfortable you are, the more comfortable he will feel. If things progress, there will be lots of chances to show your creativity.

And please don't starve yourself before the first date just because you want to look skinny in your new dress. If you haven't eaten, (a) you are going to be ravenous, (b) a few drinks are going to hit you much faster than they normally would, (c) your brain won't be sharp, and (d) your energy level will be low.

Getting to Know Each Other

Although there are some men who are eager to jump right into the deep end, most like to take new relationships day by day and date by date. Starting a serious relationship is not what most men have in mind when they meet a woman. They're more interested in an encounter, a short-term relationship or a one-night stand. Many men describe the following scenario as ideal: He will start "hanging out" with a girl, really enjoy her company, want to spend more time with her, and eventually a relationship will evolve naturally—with no pressure! Trying to rush things or setting up expectations frightens most men away. Finding the balance between being over-aggressive (jumping all over a new date like a puppy dog) and being overpassive (showing no interest and playing hard to get) on the first few dates can be crucial in developing a lasting relationship.

There is no First Date Master Recipe. Since every man and every first date is different, it's difficult to say definitively what will or will not capture his attention. Having said that, there are a number of things that will help you, and a few things that you should avoid. The most important thing to remember on your first few dates is to listen, observe, and have fun. Take this time to learn more about him and present yourself as honestly as possible.

Be Yourself

Trying to be someone other than yourself may work for a while, but it will never lead to a comfortable long-term situation. It's better to find out that you aren't compatible now than months down the road. The goal of a first date is to get to know him and see if you like him. Whatever you do, don't try to accommodate your perception of who he wants you to be. For one thing, you might be wrong. For another, it's ultimately self-defeating to mold yourself according to a man's whims. You must be yourself. This unmasked person is going to be a lot more interesting and real to him. If he doesn't like the person you truly are, it's never going to work, and why would you want a man who doesn't love and admire the real you? At this point, you don't know him and can't assume "Well, if I act this way he'll like me." So take a big breath, relax, and know that the surest way to find someone you are comfortable with is to be yourself.

How Do I Talk to Him?

On the first date you want to establish a connection and commonality. It should be fun and light. On subsequent dates you can find out more about him. For example, what does he value? Happiness, friendships, honesty, his career? Ask him what his life has been like, how he spends his time. Don't be afraid to let him start to know and understand you. If you're open and honest, he'll most likely reciprocate. Remember, on the first few dates people are often nervous. He may be also, so give him the benefit of the doubt. Take control if you need to. For instance, if the conversation is lagging, help out by asking him questions about himself or bringing up new topics, like, "What was your favorite movie?" "What do you usually do on weekends?" I've found that you can get really funny stories if you ask them about the worst date they've ever had. Even better, suggest fun places to go (e.g., for dessert or drinks). Try to find mutual interests: Ask him about his three favorite sports, albums, foods, philosophers, or books.

The key here is to pick subjects you love, so he can't go wrong with any answer. For example, if you love to travel, ask him about his three favorite destinations or where he'd most like to go. Bringing up topics that interest you is a quick and easy way of gauging whether you have common interests. Most men agree that they would rather dine with women who talk a little too much than women who have nothing to say. Nicholas wholeheartedly agreed, "On one date it was so much work to have a conversation that I had to cross the table to answer my own questions!" Plan on carrying your weight in the conversation.

Remember that people like to talk about themselves. Asking your date questions is flattering to him while also informative to you. Your tone is important. If you're friendly, open, gentle, and curious, you'll be well received. In fact, I've realized people are appreciative of talking on a more personal level.

When I asked Stan, a twenty-six-year-old engineer, about his worst first date, he had this to say. "When I asked her a straight, simple question deserving a straight, simple answer she acted coy or avoided answering. It was as if she was purposely trying to be mysterious. If she was uncomfortable giving answers to a particular question, why wouldn't she just say so? I would have preferred, 'Oh, that's a secret.' Or a joke like, 'I could tell you, but I'd have to kill you.' Anything would be better than just hanging me out on the line to dry. The questions weren't even very personal yet her reaction made me feel uncomfortable for asking the wrong thing. By being honest and frank I could have discovered something else about her—even if it was only what she wasn't comfortable discussing on a first date." I asked Stan what a woman could say if she felt uncomfortable and wanted to leave. " 'It's been great meeting you, but I'm sorry to say that I have an early meeting so I'm going to have to cut our evening short' or 'It's been a very long day, and it's time for me to head home. Thank you for taking the time to meet with me.' The most important thing is that she's polite."

There are also some excellent questions you can ask on the first few dates which may provide you with future clues about him. One friend needs to find out how much time a new man spends on the golf course. "I'll never be a golf widow again!" she says defiantly.

After a few dates, you'll often find that your conversation turns to previous dating history or significant relationships. (It's too personal for a first date and often a sensitive issue, so wait for him to bring up this topic.) If he does, try this question: What caused your significant relationships to unravel? Hang on to *every word* of his answer and think back to your wish list of what you're looking for, as well as those characteristics you find unacceptable. You may be afraid to ask bold, personal questions because you think you'll be perceived as nosy, but they take conversation to a new depth. You'll be able to decipher his capacity for one-on-one deep conversations and his sensitivity to the subject matter. If he deflects, take note.

I dated a man named Geoffrey who seemed like Mr. Amazing. Who could ask for anything more? When I asked him that question on our second date he answered, "They all complained I was emotionally distant and selfish." My ears perked up. Distant! How ridiculous! He was so open with me. Selfish? This was one of the most generous men I'd ever met! Everything else about him was perfect. Months later, it was exactly his emotional distance that broke us up. By then, I understood perfectly what they'd meant. Men will often give you all the information you need. Be careful not to spin the facts into something positive that you want to hear. Take these road signs seriously. Everyone has thresholds for intimacy—find out if yours are in the same range.

We all try to convince ourselves that little quirks or irritating habits won't affect us, but it's often precisely these things that end up driving us crazy. Pay attention to signs and clues from the beginning. If he seems too good to be true, you can ask "I can see all of the things that are great about you, but where's the catch? What are your faults?" On a first or second date you'll be amazed at what he'll tell you. Listen very carefully, not just to him, but to your own instinctive inner reactions. And always ask your questions in a nonthreatening way.

Accentuate the positive. Avoid a heated discussion on serious issues (religion, politics, your dysfunctional family) on a first date. No need to start getting into sensitive topics that could stir up negative emotions before you even know his positive qualities. After several dates, when these issues do surface, avoid having him feel like he's a steak being grilled for supper; pepper your sensitive questions with information on your own situation.

Twenty Questions

A thirty-three-year-old PFH (Potential Future Husband) whom I had dated a few times suddenly announced he was crazy about me and wanted to know everything about me. I proposed that on our next date we play a game called twenty questions. We would each come prepared to honestly answer each other's questions with the proviso that we could plead the Fifth on any three questions and they'd be automatically dropped. Although this was a scary proposition for a fourth date, I reasoned that it would be very worthwhile, since he would answer much more honestly now than in three months. What did I have to lose? Keep in mind that you'll probably be dating a few guys who fit into the SYT, MID, TM, or PFH category. These deeper questions should be reserved for the more serious men with whom you've already established a good rapport.

A deeper knowledge of his character and beliefs allows you to determine if you want to bring him into your inner circle as a friend, lover, colleague, or someone you're considering setting a friend up with. These were my questions:

1. If you had the choice of having dinner with a historian, philosopher, model, or sports star, which would you pick?

2. You're on the subway or bus on your way to work reading notes for your morning meeting, and you notice an unattractive woman on the verge of tears. Do you (a) consider it none of your business, (b) continue your work offering a "feel better" smile, (c) put your work down and try to help her in any way.

3. Do you usually just make it to a plane, or are you there well in advance?

4. In your past relationships, what were the three things women did that bothered you most?

5. What were their three biggest complaints about you?

6. On a scale of 1 to 10, how messy are you?

7. What started the worst hurt or down period of your life?

8. Who are the three people you've loved most in your life, not counting girlfriends?

9. When you are on a vacation do you prefer to lie in the sun or be active?

10. At this stage in your life, which three sports do you enjoy participating in the most?

11. Imagine it's five years from now. Look around at your ideal life and describe it to me.

12. There is a wholesale outlet thirty minutes away and a brand-name store several blocks away. Where would you consistently buy your most expensive items?

13. Are you technically minded, i.e., good with VCR hookups, car problems, etc.?

14. What religion are your parents?

15. How many times a week do you watch sports on TV?
16. On a scale of 1 to 10, how much do you like going to the movies on a date?
17. If you had a problem you couldn't resolve, would you ever ask the advice of a therapist?
18. What do you consider your worst flaw?
19. When was the last time you had sex?
20. What time do you usually fall asleep? How many hours do you usually sleep a night?

The point of asking questions along these lines is to probe the levels beyond the superficial to the deeper interests, attitudes, and philosophies that underlie a person's life. In a short period of time, you gain tremendous insights about your compatibility. You learn about his sense of responsibility, organization skills, ability to feel and express compassion, interests, energy level, values, competency, sense of self-worth, weaknesses, tendency toward external distractions, and, perhaps most important, his level of self-awareness. All this in a short discussion!

Keeping it short and fun worked well for me in this case. You might want to slip in a few of these questions yourself if you find the conversation fading. But be careful! My friend James, a financial consultant, had a disastrous experience. "I actually had this girl surprise me with a list of fifty questions on our second date. For the first five minutes I thought it was fun. As the questions turned into a serious interview, I started to get annoyed. When she started on questions about children and if I would choose my mother over my wife if they were both drowning I knew it was time to cut our date short. I felt forced to open up before I'd decided if the relationship was going anywhere."

There's a big difference between engaging him with a few questions and putting him on the hot seat. Instead of keeping it light and also answering his questions, this girl gave James no warning and had too many inappropriate personal questions too early, leaving him to feel threatened rather than amused.

Indirect Questions

Once the topic has turned personal and you feel comfortable, ask him what the ideal relationship is for him. You'll get a very good sense of where he's at emotionally and his readiness for a serious commitment. One reply might be, "Well I imagine my wife at home in our country house, a dog or two . . ." Another might say, "I'm not ready to think about anything serious but I'd like to find someone I enjoy to hang out with on the weekends."

Of course, direct questions can be very intimidating. Put yourself in his shoes. But how do you find out what stage a man is in without scaring him? If you are interested in discovering how he feels about marriage and children without asking him directly, try mentioning a couple you know who have just gotten engaged, who are "x" years old and ask him if he thinks it's too young. Clarifying where he's at is not because marriage is your primary goal but because it will influence how seriously you take the relationship. Could he someday be a PFH for you or a friend? Does he ever want to be married? You don't ever want the man to feel that your intent is to corner or trap him, so be subtle. You must measure the risk factor before ever mentioning commitment or the "M" word. And, until you've decided he's a PFH, it doesn't matter anyway.

At this point in the dating game, it's best to get marriage right out of your head. Put your focus on the man and your research, and have a great time! Is he right for you? Does he care about others? Is he good to his family? His relationship with his mother will often determine how he'll treat women. Has he grown up respecting and loving her? Does he want to spend time with her? Before you start to pant and drool like a lovesick puppy, do your homework. Take time to assess how he behaves under different circumstances. Recheck your shopping list to make sure he has the qualities you want. Of course, no man will have all of these qualities, but it is important to remember what you must have and what you're willing to compromise on.

Reading Between the Lines

Try to "listen" to his feelings in addition to what he actually says. People (men, especially) will usually tell you what you want to know if you listen closely. If you look back on first dates you've had with men in the past, you'll realize that often they told you exactly how they felt about relationships and marriage (e.g., "My last girlfriend was pressuring me for a commitment, so it ended"). Maybe you didn't hear it. Maybe you thought "Oh, that was his ex, he'll never treat me that way." Never think, "He'll change for me." Big mistake! Open your ears. He may not show you that particular side for a while, but it's there, and it may only surface once you're emotionally involved.

Don't feel badly if you've been fooled. It can happen no matter how careful or smart you are. There are men out there who purposely give an impression of themselves that is completely false. To please you or to avoid hurting you with the truth, they say exactly what you want to hear. Experience tells them what will hook you. They talk about wanting to find love and a serious relationship, when they are really not in this stage at all. Watch out for men like Rob, who tells a girl within the first few dates that he's looking to settle down and thinks she could be "the one." The girl falls quickly and hard for his gifts of flowers, romantic dinners, and talk of wanting a big family. In reality, Rob is commitment-phobic and breaks one heart after another. He's a master at getting normally cautious women to let down their guard. Remember, if he seems too good to be true he probably is. So keep your options open.

The point is, you really have to dig to figure out exactly what stage your man is in. Pick up clues from his friends, his friends' girlfriends, and your own friends' conversations with him. It can be very informative for one of your girlfriends to have a long heart-to-heart with him or one of his friends. She'll be able to tell you a lot.

Make Him Feel Comfortable

Tammy, a successful magazine editor at thirty-four, still gets the first-date jitters. "I just keep reminding myself it's only a date. There are lots more CBs where this one came from. Instead of making a big deal out of it, I concentrate on putting *him* at ease, and my own nervousness disappears." Tammy noticed that when she was relaxed and comfortable with herself, so was her date. "If I'm still noticeably uncomfortable, nervous or shy, I find the best way to handle it is to confront it directly. I just take a deep breath and tell him that I feel quite nervous." If the man has any empathy at all, he softens immediately and helps put her at ease. Tammy explained that somehow, expressing how she felt brought back her confidence. So does laughter. "Everybody likes to laugh so I'm always up on some good, relatively clean jokes. I ask him to tell me the best joke he's heard lately. Then I tell him mine."

Think of how fast an hour passes when you're talking to a good friend. If you can find the areas where you "click," the conversation will flow. If you sense he's uncomfortable, a genuine compliment will help put him at ease. "I really appreciate your [honesty/sense of humor/gentleness], it's so refreshing." Or, "I appreciate that you're a bit shy; you remind me of my favorite uncle."

Listen and Observe

The only way you can discover whether or not he embodies the qualities and personality you're looking for is by listening and observing. Being a good listener will help you get to the core of who he really is. People are often so self-absorbed thinking about their work day or future that they don't really hear what others say. Be proactive, not passive, when you listen. David, a thirty-six-year-old surgeon, told me he wants a partner who really hears and understands what he says. "It's very sexy when a woman focuses her attention on discovering me. This lets me know she's involved and interested. I can tell because she will watch me as I speak and she'll ask questions. I can't help but be drawn to women who can be in the moment and enjoy my company by genuinely reflecting on the things I talk about and vice versa. As soon as I sense she feels what I say or think is important, I open up. This is the only way she'll see who I really am and the relationship can evolve to the next level." Gather information: Find out about him, his interests, his goals, what makes him happy. Look directly in his eyes. Think: Be interested and interesting. Share your interests, too— he's trying to get to know you as well.

When you listen empathetically to anything he feels, there is emotional relief and a feeling of being appreciated. If your date is upset or bothered by his day or someone's behavior, offer to listen. Encourage him to open up and share the experience. The more he lets you know about himself the closer he will feel to you. Remember, you're still getting to know him at that point. Don't attempt to dive into his life to relieve him of past or present pain. Just be present and listen, allow him to express how he feels.

You'll need to look at a lot more than the superficial clues of where he works and what he's wearing. Watch what he does and how he behaves. Does he only talk about himself or does he ask others about their thoughts, preferences, and feelings? Does he help an elderly stranger? Give money to a homeless person? How does he talk to the waiter, taxi driver, or other people he encounters? Is he rude to them? Does he lose his temper with them? The way he addresses others is the way he might someday talk to you. Pay attention to these little things. They won't seem so little when you're on the receiving end. And remember, he's also watching your behavior. Be polite to everybody. You win no admirers by being rude and difficult.

Don't Project False Images

Sometimes women want so much for a man to match their ideal mate that they project it onto him. Patrick's entire dating strategy is built around this. He candidly explained, "With some women all I really have to do is show up. I don't say very much on purpose and wherever I leave gaps or don't take a position, the woman fills it in for me, usually with whatever *she* wants to believe. She's in my bedroom after two dates because she thinks she's found the perfect guy." The problem is *she has not been listening or observing, she has been projecting*—dreaming, imagining a truth for which there is no evidence. Watch out for this: You could find yourself with a stranger even after dating him for several months.

When you start projecting your expectations onto a man you set yourself up for a big disappointment. We all tend to think that a new man we like is much more than he actually is. We imagine his potential and make it into the reality of who he is now. Unfortunately, he may never reach that potential. When he senses you want things he can't deliver and he'll never live up to your expectations, he'll feel pressured. Instead of projecting, see and accept him for who he really is now, today. Stay out of the past and the future and live fully in the present, asking yourself how do you truly feel about him the way he is *right now*?

Accepting Him for Himself

On the flip side, even if he's not exactly what you expected or wanted, he may just be different than the other men you've known, or he may take longer to get to know. While you don't want to make excuses for his behavior, you also don't want to make rash, uninformed decisions. People can sense when they're being negatively judged; it's an awful feeling, especially when you haven't been given a decent chance.

On a first or second date, some men may come across as self-promoting braggarts or shy introverts. But remember, everyone needs time to feel comfortable. He may put what he considers to be his best foot forward on the first date. Keep an open mind and give things a chance. Be flexible in your expectations. At this point, there's no commitment on either your part or his. You always have the option of choosing not to spend any more time with him. There's never a need to hurt him, judge him, or dwell on the little things that bother you at this stage. Just concentrate on enjoying yourself. He might even end up becoming a great friend.

Put Your Best Foot Forward

Jan, a well-liked and successful businesswoman, came up with the idea of treating every date as she would her best client. Jan explained, "I go out of my way to meet at a place that's mutually convenient, I'm on time, positive, and considerate to his mood and tastes. (My preference might be quiche and salad while his is steak and potatoes.) If I have an important client who drives me crazy, instead of jumping the gun and reacting in anger, I would think about it rationally and calmly and work out a way to solve the problem. I might get mad, but I'd never yell at, insult, or stand up a client. This just makes good sense, not only with men, but with my friends and family."

For Jan this strategy isn't just for the problem times. The behavior many of her colleagues exhibit toward their best clients is more caring, polite, interested, and deferential than the behavior they exhibit to those they're close to. Unfortunately, we sometimes take boyfriends, friends, and family for granted. We feel we don't have to be on our best behavior with them. Jan says her technique worked every time. "Before each date I would tell myself, 'I'm going to treat this man as if he's the most important client I'll ever have.' My dates went unbelievably well. And even though many of them weren't Mr. Perfect, I know I made a good impression, earned his respect, and developed many lasting friendships."

Who Pays?

This is a tricky one, especially if you're initiating the date. If you plan the date, pick a reasonably priced restaurant with a great atmosphere and be prepared to pitch in. Generally, he'll offer to pick up the bill, at which point you can either accept gracefully or offer to share. Or you can graciously say, "No, let me get this, I invited you. The next time you can take care of it." This generous, polite response gives him the message you'd like to see him again. If he doesn't offer to pick up the tab on the first few dates, however, you need to consider the reasons. Is he cheap? Or is he unemployed or in school? If he's short on cash, think of ways you can help to ease the burden.

One of my friends, Bruce, inherited a substantial fortune and has always been very generous. He commented that "No matter how rich a man is, if a woman always assumes he should pay for everything, he'll feel used. I can't tell you how impressed I am when after I've taken a date out to a nice dinner she offers to pick up the movie tickets, after-dinner ice cream, drinks, or the taxi. Or, after several dates, makes me dinner. Even if she's on a tight budget, little things, like bringing a bottle of wine or renting the movie, show me she wants a balanced relationship. I'm not the only man who's very aware of these little gestures and, believe me, they go a long way." Help out. After all, it's a small price to pay for great company.

Salvaging a Disaster Date

While writing this book I was asked, "What do you do if you are out on a date and you know within the first ten minutes that you have no interest in this guy?" If a man has gone to the trouble to pick you up, take you to a nice place, and is being courteous, then he deserves the same respect. Even if he bores you to tears or there is absolutely no physical chemistry between you, you can still have a productive evening. My suggestion? Instead of focusing on the differences, focus on the things you have in common, such as friends, family, and hobbies. Ask him to share his knowledge on any topic you're interested in. You might leave completely surprised at what this seemingly boring guy has taught you. Remember, every human being has the potential to teach you something. Most important, even if he wasn't what you expected or wanted, don't forget to thank him for the evening.

Getting Stood Up

It's an awful feeling. It's happened to me three times in my years of dating. You confirm the date and time. You've set your night aside, cleaned your apartment, washed your hair, dressed, and put on your makeup. Then at the appointed time, he doesn't arrive and doesn't call. Something has come up, and, afraid of your possible wrath or his embarrassment, he bails without calling. You wait and wait and as you finally stick that Lean Cuisine into the microwave at ten o'clock, the tears start to stream down your face.

This sort of behavior shows horrific manners, extreme selfishness, and zero empathy for others. When this happens, remember the feeling so that you never resort to this behavior. No matter how uncomfortable you feel, if you've made a date and later decide for any reason you don't want to keep it, *call and let him know!* Don't be rude; treat him as you expect or hope he'd treat you. Unless it's an emergency, don't wait until an hour before to call and cancel. His time is just as important as yours.

Rudeness came back to haunt Diane. A year after she stood up Rick (she thought she'd never see him again) she fell in love with one of his best friends from college. Rick became a thorn in the relationship, telling her new love that she was self-centered and impolite. Eventually, Rick's constant negative comments ruined the relationship. It's a small world and what goes around often does come around.

Remember

- Treat him with respect.
- Let him know the real you. Isn't that who you want him to fall in love with?
- Ask questions.
- Be attentive. Listen to what he does and doesn't say.
- Help him feel comfortable with your laughter, empathy, and genuine flattery.
- Be careful not to project onto him qualities he doesn't have.
- Even if there's no romantic interest, use the evening to your advantage.
- Enjoy yourself!

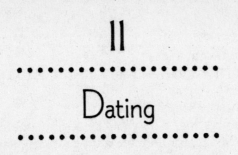

11

. . . .

Dating

. . . .

As she pushed open the door, Katie thought how happy she was to be home. It seemed like ages since she'd snuggled up with a good book on a Saturday night. While she reached for her favorite mug, she hit the play button on the answering machine. You have one message. "Hey, sweetie, I had a great time on our double date last night. What do you think of Retro-Rich's cute friend? Inquiring minds want to know. Listen, I have a date with John tonight. We're stopping by Pete's about nine o'clock so come join us if you want. Toodles." Katie smiled at the thought of Retro-Rich's tie, he still thinks it's the eighties. Anna will definitely need to give him a makeover!

Do you think there's just one perfect man for you? Or do you think there are several men with whom you could build a good life? If you believe that fate only has one Mr. Right lined up for you, then sit back and wait for him to appear. I believe in the second philosophy: Explore all the possibilities and get to know many different men. This means resisting the temptation to settle into a serious relationship with the first "acceptable" date. Compromising might seem like the solution to short-term loneliness, but your long-term happiness is at stake here. Once you start dating different men, you'll start gaining confidence and your self-esteem will rise. Automatically your standards go up. When you feel you deserve a great guy, you'll inevitably attract one. That's why over the years, boyfriends get better and better—we know what we want, and we're less likely to settle for less.

The Importance of Playing the Field

I have an important secret to share. It's time to forget about the myth that a "good girl" dates exclusively. If you want to significantly increase your dating options, then you must give yourself permission to be in the dating "driver's seat." In the 1950s, you could go to the soda shop with someone different every Friday night! If you're keeping your encounters fun and light, and everyone is having a good time, it's perfectly acceptable to date several men at the same time.

Don't waste years of your life going from one dead-end relationship to another. If you want to find the right man, put aside your settling-down impulses and keep dating many interesting men. Remind yourself of your commitment to enjoy being single. This means getting to know the guys you meet before giving your heart and body away.

Even when you've found a great date, one you consider "marriage or perfect boyfriend material," keep dating others while getting to know him better. Continue creating even more opportunities to meet PFHs. I know this goes against everything we've been taught. Usually we stick to one until disappointment slowly creeps in and spoils the romance. Even then we often hang around for some time afterward. We tend to give in to our excitement and enthusiasm about one particular man immediately and stop looking. True, we all love the feeling of a new, exciting, exclusive romance. But by letting it consume you, by immediately becoming emotionally "off the market," you limit yourself and your options.

Even if everything feels right, go slowly and be on your guard. You need to know a great deal about who a man really is, and this takes time. Don't lose your IQ just because he's gorgeous (or great in bed). Stay alert. Watch for the warning signs and don't ignore the clues. It will take time, a rational, unbiased frame of mind, and an open heart to get to know him. Getting out is hard and usually hurts, so don't tie yourself up in an exclusive relationship unless you're really sure it has long-term potential. Staying open to all the possibilities serves several purposes:

- It will help you get to know what you like and dislike in yourself and others.
- It will build your self-confidence and help you to approach new relationships from a position of strength.
- It will improve the person-to-person skills you will eventually need in a long-term relationship.
- It will make you more attractive to other men.
- And when you're eventually in a long-term relationship you won't be plagued by doubts, that little voice that says, "maybe this wasn't the right person, maybe there's someone better out there." You'll be confident about your choice and your commitment will be stronger.

Think of dating on the same terms as you would a job search. A sensible person sends out a large number of résumés and then diligently follows up on all of them. You don't usually accept the first offer you get, you wait until you have finished your other interviews and consider all of your offers. Otherwise you could lose anywhere from six months to five years in the wrong job. You don't want to be one of the many women who settled for the first man who seriously pursued them, only to wake up five years later to realize it was a mistake.

These women never got a chance to look around and evaluate their choices. They took what came to them. How do you avoid this? By not allowing one man to occupy all your thoughts, dreams, and time—and by doing a thorough, comprehensive market search before committing to a long-term relationship. This may sound coldly rational to you, but when in unknown terrain, lead with your head, not your heart; protect yourself from unnecessary pain. Many a girl has obsessed over one man who had no intention of getting serious, and in the meantime overlooked someone great. Most men run from needy, clingy, desperate women. *Do not commit* exclusively until you have done your homework.

One of my girlfriends was having problems with her boyfriend and complained to her therapist, whose response was, "At least he's *consistently* noncommittal and difficult to deal with." She reminded my girlfriend of similar bad behavior which she'd seen from the very beginning. Eight months into the relationship, my friend thought she'd found a new flaw, but in reality it was yet another personality quirk she'd overlooked because she was so hungry for a relationship.

When you are in control of your dating life and having a great time with the men of your choice, giving it all up for an average guy won't even cross your mind. The one you finally choose will be worth the wait.

Juggling Your Calendar

So you've committed to getting to know the guys who interest you and to keep going out to meet other suitable men. Give your weekdays to new MIDs (Midrange), or SYTs (Sweet Young Things), but keep your weekend nights for the PFHs (Potential Future Husbands)—you'll be more relaxed, less stressed, and you won't be in such a rush to end the date. As far as the other men you're dating are concerned, just tell them you're busy— you've got work, friends, hobbies, dates, and family obligations. It's not necessary for you to go into details regarding your social life. Some men aren't going to like this. It can be a delicate balance at times, keeping your own interests and not giving men the impression you're too busy to find time for them.

Here are a few responses for the men who prematurely pressure you: "I really like you, and I'd like to keep seeing you. When I got out of my last relationship, I promised myself that I wouldn't jump into anything too quickly," or "I really enjoy you and your company, but I'd like to take things slowly." How can he argue with this? It's just good common sense. Although most men will be delighted to find a woman with her own life, some will be jealous and resent the fact that your attention isn't focused entirely on them. Afraid that they might lose you, they will want to tie you down. Don't worry; usually this type of man will decide he wants to work harder for your love. If he pushes for a commitment too quickly, consider if he will smother your other interests, such as friends, work, hobbies, and family, or if he is potentially the one for you, long-term. If you know it will never work, be fair; let him move on.

Keep Your Interests

When you remain independent and retain power over your own life, you are exciting and enticing to a man. Jason, a very popular bachelor from Chicago, asked me, "How do women who are so active and bright when they're single—women who respect themselves and don't tolerate men pushing them around—change so radically after falling in love? I don't understand. Suddenly, they let a guy walk all over them." Many men voice this same regret. The independent, smart, strong woman they're initially attracted to changes as soon as she's in love. She loses her sense of self. Suddenly, she's staying home and making him her whole life. He's wondering what happened to the outgoing girl he fell for. He doesn't have a partner; he has a dependent. Meanwhile, he maintains his own life and wishes his girlfriend or wife had done the same.

Why should we be in the shadow of a man's job, his goals? Charlotte was a successful nurse working in a demanding Intensive Care Unit. And she looked for—and thought she had found—her White Knight. Kirkby was a powerful, good-looking corporate lawyer. When they married, Charlotte quit her job to suit his business schedule and left her time free for his convenience. Her days were spent shopping, preparing dinner, redecorating the house, and reading romantic novels. His career blossomed. Then years later, she is bitter, frustrated, and unfulfilled. She has no life of her own. Basking in his reflected glory wasn't enough for an intelligent, gifted woman like Charlotte—and it wouldn't be enough for you. Prince Charming won't fill all your needs. Only you can do that. Your personal needs and goals should not be relinquished because you find a man.

Some women think they should become more passive and let their partner make their decisions for them in order to keep the relationship. All the men I talked to, however, are looking for a woman with desires and interests of her own, someone with an opinion who can make decisions. Don't lose your voice—or your power—when you fall in love.

Don't Play Games

In general, men don't want women who play games; they want a woman who is a straight shooter. Let him fall in love with the real you. This self-honesty or integrity and authenticity should begin at your first meeting and continue throughout your relationship. Otherwise, six weeks—or worse, six months—into the relationship, he'll find out who you really are and feel deceived. Sadly, many women believe that once they've picked out the man they want to marry, the end justifies the means (i.e., trick him, fool him, manipulate him, get him by hook or by crook). This attitude is deceitful and unproductive in the long run.

It's all about getting to know each other, not about trapping him. Otherwise, even if you get the ring on your finger, he's not going to want you; he'll want the person you pretended to be. Married men complain, "She changed so much after I married her." (While married women complain that their man won't change!) The goal is to be happily married together—not to "catch a man." Dishonesty, manipulation, and deception are not the keys to a lasting relationship. Be yourself! If he doesn't like the authentic you, then go and find someone who does.

A relationship is challenging enough without having to deal with games. Tom articulated the familiar male perspective. "If a woman is constantly playing games, it may seem cute for the first few weeks. But it gets annoying very fast. You get fed up with having to trip all over yourself every single time you want to see her." Don agreed. "To get involved long-term, you don't want all that bullshit. You want to be able to be yourself, and you can't do that if she's based the relationship on games, mystery, and deception. I want to know what I'm really getting. I certainly don't want a woman who exasperates me. My wife will be interesting, someone I can talk to, who makes me feel comfortable and who's fun to be with. Someone who's supportive, honest, down-to-earth, with integrity and a sense of humor."

Don't Stop Him from Giving

There's a fine line between being independent and letting a man act gallantly. For example, my friend Tracy felt that she was proving her genuine love by turning down all the gifts her boyfriend Richard tried to shower upon her. But this was his way of showing his love. When Tracy refused to let him pay or buy her any gifts, he thought, "No matter what I do, I can't make her happy." Men don't want to feel obliged to take care of you, but they do want to feel needed and appreciated when they contribute. When a man offers to help you, opens doors, buys you a gift or flowers, show him your approval and happiness.

Men like to be asked for their advice. They like to feel that they can contribute to taking care of a woman. Don't deny them this source of satisfaction. A friend's stepdad used to bring her mother flowers every few weeks, even after they married. One time her mother made the mistake of saying, "Oh, don't waste your money bringing me flowers." She never received flowers again. Beware of being so self-sufficient or practical that men think you don't need them at all. Be your own person, but allow men to give to you, just as you give to them. They *want* to feel like your knight in shining armor. So let them! And always acknowledge and thank them for their efforts.

Myth v. Reality

In general, men are brought up to be more realistic than women. As children, while we played dress-up with our dolls or read romantic fairy tales, they were out playing sports, living in the moment, and making things happen. As a result, we often get more caught up in our fantasies than men do. We imagine the relationship as more romantic, intimate, and farther along than it is in reality. Or we think: "If Harrison Ford or Brad Pitt or the CEO of company X met me, he would fall madly in love with me, and I'd live happily ever after." Take off your rose-colored glasses; real life is far more interesting. Instead of falling in love with the dream of a relationship, fall in love with a real man.

Give Him Space

Men want to feel they have room. As Jamie put it, "I want to feel free. As long as a girl doesn't infringe on my space, I'll keep calling. Dates are a time to unwind. I'm not looking to run a difficult marathon. I just want a fun, easygoing relationship with whomever I date and hopefully someday with my wife. My last girlfriend just assumed we'd be together for dinner or that I was spending the night. She constantly judged my friends and told me what to do. If she was dying to know more about my personal life, putting me on the hot seat about who, when, and where was not the way to do it. I decided we both had a right to our own freedom—from each other."

Unspoken Attitudes

Even if you are only *thinking* something that's threatening to a man, he'll pick it up. If you're hoping and dreaming this man will fall in love with you or ask you to marry him, unconsciously you'll be acting very differently than if you're thinking, "I love spending time with this guy but I'm not sure what the future holds." I know it's a tall order to change the way you think, but if you can, it may dramatically alter the way you relate to each other. It helps to understand what men are afraid of.

His Fear: Being swallowed up and having you take over.
Your Solution: Have and keep your own life.
His Fear: Being responsible for your happiness.
Your Solution: Be self-sufficient! Make yourself happy.
His Fear: Being pushed into a commitment.
Your Solution: Keep your options open, keep dating others, and keep the word "commitment" out of the conversation.
His Fear: Being trapped.
Your Solution: Encourage him to enjoy his own time and friends and show him that you're as independent as he is.

With these in mind, watch your nonverbal signals. If he feels you're simply enjoying his company with no undercurrent of pressure, he'll assume that you're still deciding, and he will naturally keep working for your love. You'll be a desired addition to his life, not a "ball and chain." When you live for a man, he feels threatened. But when you live for yourself, he's attracted.

Jake unconsciously sabotaged the relationship every time he felt Andrea was getting too close. If they'd had a particularly intimate week together, and everything was going great, he would do something to upset her or push her away. Continual closeness and intimacy scared him; this was his way of stepping back, of slowing down the speeding train. To him the train was headed for the abyss, where he might not be able to control his emotions. So Jake put on the brakes. Of course, this started an unfortunate chain reaction. As Jake pulled back, Andrea's self-doubt crept in, and her instinct was to hold on tighter. But this was exactly the time for Andrea to take a step back and give him some air. Remember, for many men withdrawal is a natural process, so don't let it drive you crazy. Trust his feelings for you and let him have his space. Use the time to focus on yourself and your goals, expecting that absence will make his heart grow fonder.

When you're happy, comfortable, and secure within yourself, you'll be able to allow the man you love the freedom to pursue what makes him happy. By giving him freedom, you might run the risk of losing him. But you're much more likely to lose him if you hold him so close that he can't breathe. When he feels you support him in being his own person, he'll love you all the more.

Know When to Fold

Don't waste your time on anybody who doesn't know they want you. I asked the guys what the signs were when they no longer cared. Here's what they told me. "I start to take her for granted and limit my effort to the bare minimum. I don't call when I'm late or plan for the next date. When she brings up any of the above I have no excuse and I don't even care that she's upset. When the physical relationship starts to fizzle and I no longer want to have sex with her it's a sure sign that I don't care anymore." When a man cares, he'll meet you halfway or go out of his way. He should want to be with you as much as you want to be with him. If he's putting in no effort, fold your cards and walk away.

Remember

- Dating is an essential part of becoming aware of your options and getting to know yourself and your needs.
- Don't allow one man to dominate your life until you've really explored all the possibilities.
- Be proud of who you are. This will interest him much more than playing the hard-to-get game.
- Individual interests and outside activities are what make us attractive to other people, including our mates.
- Work as a team: Take an interest in and encourage his projects and ambitions.
- Be who you are—and stay who you are.
- There are too many good men out there to waste time on the ones who don't appreciate you.

12

. . . .

Top Fifteen Things Women
Do That Turn Men Off

. . . .

Gossiping

Criticizing other women's looks or intelligence is a type of female combat, a way to verbally eliminate the competition. For some, it's a favorite sport. However, Peter, a major catch, captured the sentiments of almost every man I spoke to when he admitted, "I don't feel comfortable with women who sit around bad-mouthing others. It makes her look small and petty. I hate it. And I can tell you that it's certainly not a trait my future wife will have!"

Gold Digging

No man wants to think his wallet is the main attraction. And many men feel that questioning them about what they do is the same as asking them how much money they make.

As one friend put it, "Some women don't seem to care what a man's name is, just where he works and what his W-2 says. They want expensive meals or gifts, not the man and his company."

Sometimes it isn't necessarily what you say but what you wear that gives the impression you might be interested only in the material side of life. Caryl wears so much jewelry that one arm hangs lower than the other from the weight of all of her bracelets and rings. Even for a casual movie date, she's loaded down with jewels. Paul told me, "I felt intimidated and uncomfortable. How could I live up to what's important to her?"

Nagging or Criticizing

No one likes to be criticized. Just think how you feel when somebody is constantly pointing out where you've stumbled and how he or she could have done things better. Instead of criticizing, use honesty softened with understanding and compassion: "When you do that, Dave, I feel my body getting tense, and it immediately triggers my angry button. I'm sure this isn't your intention, but this is the response I have." He'll be less offended if you put it in terms of how *you* feel rather than criticizing *him*. Nobody's perfect and everybody needs love and assurance. If you can only love a perfect man, you're going to be very lonely.

Hanging on Too Tight

Some women cling to men for dear life. They can't pick a movie or restaurant without his advice. They rely on him to fix or solve all of their problems. They depend on a man for everything and need him to call several times a day. This drives men crazy. It's like having gum on their shoe, a responsibility that only interrupts their stride. Men need their energy to move their own lives forward. It's not their job to "save" you. *Save yourself!*

Jealousy

When Andy was out and about going to bars or parties with his friends, he met many girls. Instead of having the confidence that Andy wasn't going to meet anyone he cared for more, Laurel let her jealousy get in the way of a solid two-year relationship. "She questioned my every move and even the numbers on my long-distance phone bill. I loved her dearly and was completely faithful, but her paranoia eventually killed the relationship." Laurel lost a potentially valuable relationship. Put yourself in Andy's shoes. Imagine dating a man who's so insecure that every time you're out with your friends or talk to another man, he's afraid you'll leave him. Wouldn't you start to wonder why he didn't think he was special enough for you?

Jealousy is self-defeating. Dwelling on these feelings lowers self-confidence and makes you feel helpless, angry, resentful, trapped, and inadequate. Besides, ungracious behavior implies that you don't wish the best for people. Wish happiness for yourself, but don't begrudge it for anyone else. The best way to stay close to a man is to give him his freedom. If he's trustworthy, fight back that green-eyed monster and give him a break. If he gives you no reassurance in the relationship or if you know he's cheating, then it's time to give the relationship a break and move on.

Not Saying Thank You

Men hate it when they go to the trouble of arranging a date, picking a woman up, taking her out for a nice dinner, movie or show, spending money and, at the end of the evening, not even receiving a thank-you. Bill, twenty-eight, explained, "It's not the money, it's the principle. If I'm going to take the trouble to treat her like a lady, she should at least make the effort to act like one. A sincere thank-you goes a long way." Bill said he would never forget the time he took Pam out for her birthday early in their relationship. "I knew she loved jazz so I planned drinks at a great jazz club and dinner at one of the best restaurants in town. Before dessert she excused herself from the table to make a call. When I got home there she was on my machine. 'I'm in the middle of dinner with the most amazing, thoughtful guy, and I just wanted to say I wouldn't want to spend my birthday any other way.' I was really touched. I can pinpoint this as the moment I started to fall in love with her." If he was particularly thoughtful or made a special effort, drop him a note or call just to say thanks.

Insecurity

Men are comfortable with women who are comfortable with themselves. When a man compliments you, he hopes you'll accept it and thank him. Jim complained to me about his college girlfriend, Hillary. "Every time I compliment her on how nice she looks it opens up a bevy of insecurities. 'This dress makes me look fat' or 'I need to lose some weight' or 'I can't believe my face chose *this* night to break out.' I never would have noticed any of those things," he said, "unless she pointed them out." This kind of thinking is self-defeating and denigrating to him. Not accepting a compliment is equivalent to saying you think he has bad taste. If you don't know your own worth how can he? *When you believe in yourself, he will believe in you.*

Insecure women are continually concerned and worried about how to behave, what to wear, and how they look. Or as Don, an Internet entrepreneur, notes, "The most annoying question is 'What should I wear?' or 'You remember my black dress with the gold buckle?' Let's be serious, the only dresses I'm going to remember are the ones cut down to her navel. When I call a women and ask what to wear, all I need to know is, do I have to wear a tie or a jacket?" Uncertain about what to wear? Ask another woman. If you need to know how to dress call the restaurant or event coordinator.

Chronic Complaining and Whining

For chronic complainers and whiners, nothing is ever right. Their glass is perpetually half empty. If you complain to the man you're dating, it will turn him off. That's why you have your diary. Not only is a woman who complains all the time unpleasant to be around, she emits high-pitched sounds that scream to a man "high-maintenance." He feels he'll be expected to solve all of her problems. One thing I know for sure, an optimist is always going to have a better life than a pessimist.

Smoking

Almost all of the nonsmoking men I spoke to said this was one of the biggest turnoffs. "If she smokes, I'll take her home, but I won't date her." Besides making you smell like an ashtray, it decreases lung capacity, causes cancer, and prematurely ages your skin. If you do smoke, ask if he minds and never light up when he's eating.

Dwelling on Past Relationships: Yours or His

Many men assume that if a woman talks endlessly about her past relationships, she's either hinting that she's not really interested in him or is not yet over her latest ex. Either way, they consider it a sign of unneeded baggage. Men can also feel uneasy, threatened, or vulnerable when asked to divulge the intimate details of their own past relationships. While this information can indeed be helpful, don't force him to talk about something—or someone—until he's ready. No matter how anxious for information you are, be patient and respect his privacy, particularly in the early stages of the relationship.

Babbling

Some women chatter on and on in exquisite detail about superficial things like where they bought their makeup, what their hairdresser said, or what someone was wearing. Meanwhile, their date politely pretends he's interested while completely tuning out. Don reiterated the harsh truth. "If she comes across as an airhead I might stick around for a few dates, because she looks good. But my goal will be to get her into bed, not to have any kind of lasting relationship. At least in bed, she won't bore me to death. I don't know a heterosexual man alive who wants to hear about where she got her nails done, what kind of purse she bought, or what kind of new makeup she's wearing. We're just not interested."

Men may initially show an interest to be nice or keep you engaged in conversation, but many guys describe this mindless banter as "painful." As Dan, a twenty-two-year-old grad student, put it, "I just don't need to hear about her pet that died when she was in high school." Don't alienate him; engage him. Find something newsworthy, funny, or philosophical to discuss—anything is better than talking about girl stuff. Save that for your girlfriends. Don't be afraid to let him see you have a brain. Any self-respecting man wants a bright girl-friend; especially if he'll eventually consider her as the mother of his children.

Not Unlocking His Car Door

A secret test passed down from father to son, brother to brother. "Unlock her door first and then see if she leans over to unlock yours. If she doesn't it's a sure sign that she's selfish."

Traveling with a Busload of Suitcases

Overpacking is the sign of a prima donna who expects traveling companions to carry bags for her. If it can't fit into a pull-along carry-on and one smaller tote bag, leave it at home. Some tips for traveling light: Create a small cosmetics bag, filled with everything in miniature size. Never take anything you don't always wear at home (you won't wear it while away, either). Stick to two pairs of shoes (casual and evening). If both are black, they can be worn with any color combo. Bring clothes that pack easily, like cottons and knits.

Staking out Territory

When we landed on the Moon, we planted a flag. That's how women feel about men's apartments. They establish it as their territory by leaving a mark to stake their claim, to show that they've been there. As one friend lamented, "Women have eagle eyes. If another woman leaves something, a scarf or an earring, a man won't notice it for days. But another woman will spot it within two seconds." Men who are just casually dating get upset when women mark their territory prematurely. They resent the woman who caused the trouble. Don't purposely leave things at his house until he implies it's okay.

Keeping Him Waiting

Matt was one of the many men who had this on the top of his list of dislikes. With great enthusiasm he declared, "A man would never dream of keeping a bunch of people waiting while he put gel in his hair or groomed his beard. Yet you often hear women saying, 'But I'm putting on my makeup,' or 'I'm blow-drying my hair,' as if these are good reasons to keep anybody waiting for forty-five minutes. Falling down the steps and breaking your ankle is a good reason to keep people waiting, but primping isn't." The irony of this is men prefer natural-looking women over heavily made-up women. "Too done" smacks of high-maintenance.

If you learn how to do the fifteen-minute, or at most, half-hour version, think of all the extra time you'll have for the important things in life, like working toward your goals, helping a friend, reading a good book, or dating. It's crazy to miss three-quarters of a party because you're applying one more coat of mascara. Nobody is going to notice it except you. Meanwhile, you're missing out on all the fun.

PART IV

· · · · · · · · · · · · · · · · · · · ·

The Relationship

13

• • • • • • • • • • • • • • • • •

Communication

• • • • • • • • • • • • • • • • •

Scrolling through her E-mail, Katie's thoughts turned to the weekend. Anna's message flashed on the screen. "Am I on a roll or what? Retro-Rich has tickets for us to see Cher on Friday night, John promised me a candlelit dinner on Saturday, and on Sunday I have brunch with Feisty Frank (don't ask . . . LOL). Give Louise a call, you might be able to pry her loose from Dave. I sense there's trouble in paradise, they don't seem to be on the same disk drive these days. XOXO Anna."

Whether you're dating casually or ready to narrow the field to one special guy, how you relate will determine the quality of your communication and the relationship.

Rachel believed she needed to mask her true feelings and present a pleasing—but not necessarily genuine—facade in her quest for a mate. But by not allowing her true self to emerge, she buried her own needs. Her boyfriend, Dan, smoked cigars. Rachel hates smoking, but when Dan asked if it bothered her, she replied, "Oh, I don't mind at all." She knew Dan loves sports. Although she has no interest, she told him how much she loved mountain biking, hiking, and skiing. Thinking Rachel would love a challenging outdoor adventure, Dan organized a surprise trip to Outward Bound, a wilderness adventure program. Rachel couldn't hide her frustration and misery as she longed for her warm, comfortable apartment. By the end of the trip the relationship was over. Pretending to be someone else only led Rachel to heartbreak. What if she'd waited until she'd snagged, bagged, and married him before showing her true self? Dan would soon find he'd married an actress. And since their relationship had been built on pretense, he'd find true intimacy unattainable. Dan admitted, "She would have gained so many more points by being herself. I would have planned a trip more in line with both our interests and we'd probably still be together."

We all know that good communication isn't always easy between the sexes. If you want to understand each other better, you'll both need to sharpen your communication skills.

Here's how to get started.

Be Honest

By pretending, you're not only being unfair to your mate, you're cheating yourself. Love takes time to grow, and honesty is a key ingredient. It encourages trust. And where there's trust, love flourishes. This doesn't mean you have to spill your guts and tell him on the first date the intimate details of your life. A little mystery is enticing. But you should always be as honest as possible. Instead of fabricating who you think he wants you to be, reveal yourself. Men sense when you have a hidden agenda or if something isn't authentic. You can be sure that most men will bolt when they start to feel you're not what you appear to be. To be his equal, his best friend, you'll need to communicate openly. This builds the tight bonds to help you keep a friend, a lover, and a husband.

If you're spending extra time and energy pretending you're someone else, you're missing out on the freedom and excitement of letting go and being your true self. When you open up, you (and those around you) will feel free and uninhibited. It may shock you that the real you, the one you've been so carefully concealing, is the very woman he finds most appealing.

Beth, a twenty-one-year-old student, knew Gordon loved working out, so she went to the gym to see him every day. Actually, indoor athletics bored her. She much preferred running on an open field or biking against the wind. One day, in an offhanded comment, she mentioned this to Gordon. It turns out he was training for the Ironman Triathlon. He jumped at the chance of having a training partner. They spent the next weekend biking together. Their relationship sped around the corner from friendship to romance.

Nurture Each Other

As you narrow down the dating field and begin dating more seriously or even exclusively, communication will become more meaningful. In truly great relationships, people nurture each other. They grow together. What enables them to do this? Listening and paying attention to each other's needs. If you want your mate to know your dreams and desires, express them, and allow him to express what he needs from you. By encouraging and uplifting the person you love, together you can make the difficult times seem less overwhelming. A nurturing relationship requires that you both pitch in, roll up your sleeves, and share the bad times as well as the good.

Soon after the stock market plummeted and jobs were scarce, David, a popular New York bachelor, lost his high-paying job. In the next few months spent in the job search, his girlfriend, Janine, kept him focused on his own self-worth. Her confidence in him held firm; the crisis was actually a catalyst for bringing them closer. It provided the opportunity for Janine to stand by his side and offer a nonjudgmental ear and her support. Impressed by her genuine love and loyalty, two months after he started his new job he took her to Key West, and as they watched the sunset, he asked her if she would marry him.

The story of my girlfriend Andrea and her fiancé, Bob, also comes to mind. When I watch them interact, sometimes I can't help but roll my eyes. On an hourly basis she coos, "How on earth did you ever figure that out? Oh Bobby, you're the smartest man in the whole world." She continually compliments him on the way he navigates through traffic, his food choices, the clothing he wears, and oh yes, let's not forget his superhuman sexual powers. Of course he relishes all this praise and returns her generosity with compliments, gratitude, and love. As nauseating as this might seem to an observer, I've never seen a couple bounce back faster from arguments. By appreciating every little thing, they've trained themselves never to take each other for granted.

Everyone draws happiness from being admired and appreciated, especially by those they love. Encourage your mate to live up to his full potential by promoting his positive qualities and gestures. "I really love you for being so supportive." "Have I told you lately how wonderful you are?" said lightly with a quick kiss, can reaffirm your support. You'll find that when misunderstandings do arise, your positive daily attitude will act as a strong buffer. This is not meant as a manipulative tactic, rather as a way to express your gratitude with sincere compliments.

But remember, nobody can ever fill a void within you for self-love. First you must nurture yourself before you can nurture another. Otherwise, instead of filling you up, nurturing someone else will seem like a drain.

No, He Can't Read Your Mind

How many times do our girlfriends say, "He should *know* how I feel!" or "I shouldn't have to ask him." Unfortunately none of us are mind readers; we need to be told. Any successful relationship requires constant, open, honest communication about what you're feeling and thinking.

It takes courage to say, "What you said bothered me" or, "That hurt my feelings." Or simply "Excuse me," with an upward inflection that suggests the speaker rethink what they have just said. So instead of responding directly, many women play games. They may get upset over other things, pretend nothing's wrong, or stay silent. Meanwhile, their partner has no idea what's going on. He becomes increasingly frustrated.

Pretty soon there's a full-blown argument based solely on mis-communication or sarcasm! By being straight and saying "I feel hurt and sad," you give him the opportunity to apologize and explain or discuss the situation. There's nothing to fear if you're direct, kind, and clear.

Just remember, it's all in the delivery. Instead of demanding, ask. Instead of whining, explain. Instead of criticizing, comment. Ask yourself, "Does he want to hurt me? Or is he just reacting because he's hurt? Does he want the relationship to dissolve?" If the answer is no, then focus on finding a solution. In this situation you have nothing to lose by opening your heart. If your answer is yes, then think about getting out!

Eric, an architect in his early thirties, had this complaint. "Just because my girlfriend doesn't like something doesn't mean I should go without. Some things are really important to me, like riding my motorcycle with the guys, and she'll never understand, since it's not important to her. But I never complain when she goes shopping or talks on the phone for hours."

It's also unrealistic to expect partners to give equally at the same time. At any given time, it may be more like 80/20. By practicing patience and fairness, by being there for him when he needs you, hopefully, he'll be there for you. But don't give because you want or expect something in return, or you'll set yourself up for disappointment. Romantic relationships are not about the exchange of goods and services, they are about the exchange of energy and love. To maintain a good relationship you'll need to balance each other's needs.

Tackle Problems Early

Have you seen how fast a brushfire spreads? Train yourself to catch potential conflicts when they're still just a spark. It's much easier to address little problems than bigger ones. If you're upset or hurt about something, don't carry it around.

By sweeping it under the rug you allow something small to become much bigger than it should be.

My friend Patrick, a thirty-two-year-old lawyer, had this to say: "Every time my ex was mad she'd yell. Her whiny voice was like listening to nails on a blackboard. I knew I was partly to blame for blanking out the message, but subsequently our relationship never improved. I also knew I could never marry someone who was unable to express herself calmly and rationally." As tensions and emotions mount, the real issues often become clouded. When somebody upsets us, our first reaction is to lash out and argue back. Stop the argument right there. Calmly douse the fire. It takes patience, practice, and discipline to use a tone of voice that keeps others engaged and listening. An earnest, moderate voice no louder than if you were asking someone the time of day works. No one listens or hears very well in a yelling match.

Once again, imagine yourself in a business situation. Say you have a problem in negotiating with a company or a client. You'd calmly list the points you disagree with and then either compromise or lose the deal. Why wait for a conflict? When things are going well, suggest that you both make a list of five little things and five big things that bother you. By honestly addressing your needs you can both start to find solutions. Start by discussing the small things, then tackle the tougher ones. Be prepared to push back your initial instinct to react with anger, tears, or defensiveness. To move the relationship to a deeper level you'll need to negotiate problems with a clear head.

You might say, "I can change X and Y easily, can you be patient while I work on the hardest thing, Z?" Just by reading his list, you'll learn a great deal about his wants and needs and vice versa. "You're never on time, I don't like your perfume, you let the dishes pile up in the sink, you spend more time on the computer than with me. You never come to my neighborhood for dinner—I always seem to come to yours. You haven't made an effort with my friends." On a few of his points you'll probably find yourself saying, "I didn't even know that bothered you. I'd be happy to change it" or, "I actually thought you liked it." Don't simply be satisfied that you've both aired your woes. This is an opportunity to understand him better and to contribute to a solution. You don't need to fix everything all at once. Resolving these issues rationally, fairly, and empathetically keeps the relationship healthy—and moving forward.

The "Right" Way to Fight

Every relationship must have an outlet for conflict. If there's never any conflict or disagreement, ask yourself if you're suppressing your needs. You may be sacrificing yourself to appease others. Since disagreements are inevitable, learning the art of how to fight fair is imperative. Just because you're upset and angry doesn't mean you can stop respecting and caring about others. The way you approach these problems will make or break the relationship. Here are some guidelines to prepare you for those difficult but sometimes necessary times.

The Relationship Is More Important Than the Fight

A relationship can run along smoothly for years, yet when an altercation occurs, one person can walk away. Years of good will vanish as they are consumed with the disagreement at hand. *The strength of every relationship hinges on how conflict is negotiated.*

You may disagree with him. You may, in fact, be furious. But don't let things fall apart over something small and petty. My girlfriend Cindy actually broke up with her boyfriend over a fight based on who hogged the remote control. Insults started flying. She called him a selfish pig, he called her a controlling bitch, and war was declared. Maria, a twenty-seven-year-old makeup artist, handles conflict with her guy another way. "I remind myself that he has been there for me on many occasions and he's added a lot of value to my life. I imagine that on a higher level, I'm committed to the relationship. I think of it as something I don't want to tear down, which is exactly what fighting the wrong way will do." As Maria explained, "When I feel like pushing him away, I constantly remind him and myself that the relationship is much more important than this isolated incident."

Tell yourself that his point of view is just as important to him as yours is to you. The goal in a fight is to communicate and grow, not be the victor. Remember, if one partner loses, ultimately you both lose.

Be Direct

When you're upset, instead of complaining to your girlfriends, bad-mouthing your guy, and adding fuel to the fire, confront the problem head-on. Rather than gathering others to support your position, talk directly with him. Ask him, "Are you upset about [X]?" or "I felt sad when you did [Y]." If you solve problems together, your bond will strengthen rather than weaken. If you find yourself becoming distant and unreachable, come back. Only by being fully present and communicating your fears and needs will the relationship grow. Most men don't want to argue. They want to know what you need help with and they prefer to have a choice.

Everyone wants to feel they're in control of their own decisions. My friend Jane, a thirty-year-old editor, faced this with her Italian boyfriend. She yearned for him to improve his English. And she also wished he'd partake in some of her favorite activities: opera, parties, movies, reading. Instead of bombarding him with requests to change, she asked him to focus on one thing and gave him a choice. He decided to improve his English. This gave him a sense of control and confidence. To Jane's surprise, he began exploring her other interests. The language gap had been holding him back all along. They solved their differences and grew together.

Create a Safe Environment

Most people want to avoid the pain of confrontations. Ed, an easygoing thirty-three-year-old in the insurance business, told me, "I'll walk out of the room or even leave the house if I'm confronted by anger or hysteria. This approach accomplishes nothing with me. I don't know any guy who responds well to overt challenge, except maybe a few lawyers who enjoy the thrill of a battle."

If you need to have a serious talk with him, don't whack him over the head with it. Arrange a good time for both of you. The right time is not at the office where he can't talk, or after you know he's had a bad day, in the middle of his favorite show, at 2:00 A.M., or after you've been drinking.

Obviously, you want him to listen with compassion, and you want to evaluate his performance. To accomplish this, you must help him feel safe. Let him know you love him and that you're not going to run away, just because a sensitive issue has arisen. Start with the positive: "You know how much I value your love and our friendship." Remember, it's not *him* (you love him); it's what he is *doing* that's bothering you. Telling him what to do won't work. Expressing how you *feel* may. "Honey, I'm reluctant to mention this but it's been grating on me for a while. The odor of your jogging clothes and sneakers upsets me. I find myself getting resentful because I can't believe you don't notice how bad the smell is and do something about it." He needs to make the decision to change his behavior. After you've aired your grievances, always thank him for listening. Likewise, he wants to know that his feelings count, too. To accomplish this, actively listen to him and then demonstrate that you heard by repeating what you think he means. For instance if he says, "You know how late I get home from work, I just don't have time to do laundry until the weekend." You might respond "I know how little time you have and I'm empathetic to how hard you work and that you're tired. But could you put your jogging clothes some place other than the bedroom floor? Is there a possibility you could buy a hamper and put it in the closet or take things to the Laundromat downstairs?"

Often, men take a hard line when you've hurt their feelings. You have to develop a plan to avoid hitting this wall. Balance expressing your feelings with appreciation for his existing qualities. For example, "There are so many wonderful things you do. I was wondering if you could do one more thing: put the toilet seat down so I don't fall into it in the middle of the night." Remember, always request, never demand. Ask him with the same tone you would use for your best client. After all, he's far more important than any client! And always let him know you love him. Instead of saying "You're a jerk when you do that" try, "When you behave this way I feel [hurt/sad/taken advantage of]." (He can't argue with how *you* feel.)

The key is to use a gentle, calm voice in expressing your true feelings and to be willing to make the conversation a two-way street. Show him you're also willing to work on the issues and change. This will be the biggest incentive for him to work on himself. Because unless he wants to change, no amount of pushing from you can make him. For example, Sara, a thirty-one-year-old professor, always felt let down when her boyfriend of four years, William, forgot special events like Valentine's Day. One year after calling him an insensitive, thoughtless, birdbrain she decided to plan ahead. She found his office date book and put all the important dates in big red letters. His mother's birthday, her birthday, their anniversary . . . A week before Valentine's Day she also dropped a subtle, positive hint. As they passed a deli with flowers she said "I love having flowers around the house." It gave William a clear signal what she wanted—and you can bet that year he followed through.

Listen to His Point of View and Isolate the Issues

If he's upset, listen to him. Hear the message, not the emotion. Jamie, a twenty-four-year-old musician, wants to know that his girlfriend, Heather, understands. "I want her to hear my complaint and know she cares about how I feel. Unless she acknowledges my anger, I'll keep expressing it. As soon as I know she understands my perspective, my hostility immediately diffuses." Instead of saying "You're wrong" or taking a stand to entrench yourself, be willing and flexible enough to listen to his ideas and the feelings behind them. Complete honesty about what's really behind the issue, delivered kindly, will establish trust and set the stage for a cooperative discussion.

Although I have more physically stunning friends than Sonya, the greatest guys always gravitate toward her, hoping they might get a chance to date her. Most of my single male friends have delegated her a saint. What makes Sonya so special is her ability to empathize. She always seems truly tuned-in to what others feel. And men can't get enough of her. As her current significant other explained, "I feel like she really hears what I say and accepts me. I guess I'm grateful for her compassion." Instead of blaming, fixing, or controlling the guys she's dated, Sonya gives them her full understanding. Her empathy encourages their trust and they quickly open up to her on a deep level.

If there are problems you both need to tackle, lay them out rationally, empathetically and one at a time. Gather as much information as you can to determine what's upsetting each of you. Listen compassionately to his grievances without interrupting and then let him know the core feelings upsetting you. "I didn't tell you that because I'm afraid you might leave me if I speak my mind." "I reacted that way because I felt you cared more about her than you do me. I was jealous." Both of you must be able to share your concerns in a safe way and have your feelings validated.

For example, my friend Janice lives with her loving boyfriend, Ned. He works at an investment bank and is under constant stress. When he comes home, Ned wants a half hour or so to himself. "It's my time to unwind," he explained. By contrast, Janice, who works in a quiet library, is full of energy. "I want to share my day with him. It hurts when he shuts me out." So while Ned tries to watch television, Janice stands there and chats. They both get frustrated. The solution? Ned needs to explain to Janice that he's not rejecting her. He truly needs downtime. And after he's relaxed he needs to make an effort to give her the time she needs to connect. He needs to honestly let her know where he's coming from. "I really do want to talk about your day, I just need some time to unwind." This way, they're both being respectful, sympathetic, and responsive to each other's needs.

Isolating issues also means using discretion as to whether to raise a concern. Arguments do happen, but make sure the issues you fight over are valid. Like the boy who cried wolf, if you explode over petty concerns, he won't listen to what's important. You want him to hear you not dismiss you. Bring things to his attention, certainly, but it's not worth overdramatizing and provoking arguments about little things. He's not perfect, and neither are you. For example, religious beliefs or political persuasion may be important and difficult issues. But hairs left in the sink are fairly minor.

As you tackle each problem be sure not to cloud the issues by overwhelming him with multiple non-related issues from the past. As Jamie explained, "My girlfriend's like the elephant that never forgets. She brings out the same list of my past failures every time we argue. It's totally unproductive." Pick your battles wisely. Don't let the little things take on more importance than your love.

Make Sure You Understood What Was Said

When I was a child we played a game called "Telephone." A group of friends sat around in a circle and whispered a message from one person to the next. By the time the message reached its originator, it had changed dramatically. It's the same in arguments. People may hear what you say, but they hear it filtered through their own life experiences, emotions, insecurities, issues, or opinions. They often perceive things differently than you intended. As the game of telephone shows, the same sentence can mean five different things to five different people.

Pam's story also illustrates this. She and her boyfriend, Rick, were arguing about her need to feel more cared for. She blurted out a small side comment mentioning that he never dressed nicely for her. What Pam meant was, "I wish you would go out of your way for me more often." Instead, Rick took it as a sign that she didn't like his clothes. The next time they argued, he got up and actually started changing his shirt. It dawned on Pam how literally he'd interpreted her comment. "It was such a funny, thoughtful gesture," she said, "even though we were fighting, he was trying to please me. I laughed so hard I forgot what we were fighting about." Rick later explained to me, "Men say what they mean. Once, before we moved in together, we had an argument. Pam told me not to call her. I thought she meant it and didn't call, thinking I'd upset her even more. It turned out she was much more upset that I didn't call her than about the fight itself."

Make sure you say what you mean and that you understand what he's saying. Repeat his argument calmly and ask if you understand it correctly. You might inquire, "Are you saying such-and-such?" After listening to his complaint or concern and letting him know you understand, together you can find a way to resolve it. These situations can be very difficult. Instead of reacting defensively, try to hear and absorb his point of view. Try to *share* the responsibility.

Temper, Temper

What about the times when you're so upset you just want to scream? These are the real tests of love. Yes, you have a valid point. And yes, you want to get it across. However, as soon as you raise your voice or lose your temper, he'll stop listening. Neil, a thirty-two-year-old hotel manager, put it this way. "All I sense is danger, that what she's saying is negative and painful. My walls go up. She'll be blasting away, and I'll be busy deflecting what she says, protecting myself, thinking about my comeback, trying to counter her anger and probably losing my temper as well. I certainly won't be empathizing with her feelings." So above all, use a nonthreatening tone. Speak from your core not your ego. When you get your point across, you both win.

In truth, a bad temper is a symbol that old wounds have been reopened by the present circumstances. Nobody should have to be subjected to a spoiled, uncontrolled adult who's screaming or turning blue in the face. It is an ugly sight and accomplishes absolutely nothing except to show that this person has a lot of work to do on themselves. If you find yourself flaring up, step back and take a moment to collect yourself or institute a policy of time-outs to defuse emotions on both sides.

Remember, no one ever really wins a fight. In fact, you lose a lot more than just your temper when you yell. Think about the times when someone screamed at you. The message you heard was, "To hell with you! It's my way or no way. I'm not going to listen or even consider your point of view!" If you have a tendency to lose your temper, learn to say "I'm not going to say anything right now, because if I do, it will be full of anger. I'd rather talk when we've both calmed down." Others don't *make* you angry. *You* make yourself angry.

If he loses his temper, ask him questions. "What's your objective with this conversation? Is this the optimal way for us to be communicating?" "Do you think it would be helpful if we took a five-minute break?" An angry person immediately becomes more rational if they have to switch off their emotions and think about answering your questions. Or try listening without interrupting. He'll finish letting off steam faster and then you can focus on solving the problem. Or try saying, "I'm sorry you're upset. I really want to know how you feel, but I can't respond when you're yelling." It's amazing how saying "you're right" and not adding any excuses or buts can defuse a situation.

In a heated argument you can choose to be warlike and hostile or search the turmoil to find peace and love. It might help to imagine Mother Teresa on one shoulder and Saddam Hussein on the other. The next time you're in a fight, realize that you have a choice.

Tit for Tat

Instead of asking herself if she'd contributed to a problem and putting her energy into changing her own negative patterns, Margaret would play tit for tat. Even when she knew she was wrong, she'd never admit it. Instead she'd deflect her wrongdoing by bombarding her target with a laundry list of hurtful things saved up for such an occasion. She would go to great lengths to dig up and manipulate evidence to support her position and stir up her opponent's emotions. Each zinger was meaner than the last. "You should hear what your so-called friend Esther had to say about you!" Margaret thought a fight could only be won by trickery and cruelty. What she never realized was that conflict is only won with love.

Remember, the only person you can truly change is yourself. Consider that others' behavior may play off yours and work on changing yourself first. If you tell a significant other "I don't like it when you do [X]," he'll probably come back and say, "I behave that way because you do [Y]." A lot of arguments stem from tit-for-tat spats where blame gets tossed around like a Ping-Pong ball. Stop throwing the blame back. When you change your own behavior, you'll usually find he'll change his response.

Make sure that if you confront him, you also confront yourself. When you both stop pointing fingers and begin expressing what you truly feel, growth and real bonding begins. If you're having trouble apologizing, write a note or do something thoughtful to let him know you're sorry. The reward of practicing your communication skills will be healthy, happy, long-lasting relationships. Maintaining a happy relationship requires real work.

If you're spending all your time arguing, analyzing, or discussing the relationship, then you've stopped participating in it. Romance should bring happiness, not seem like a second job. At some point you need to ask if this problem is a detour, a flat tire, or if it's time to get off the highway to hell.

Remember

- When you stop communicating the relationship stops developing.
- You love him, so empathize.
- Tell him you think the relationship is worth the effort to communicate and resolve your differences.
- Let him speak uninterrupted—and ask him to listen without interrupting you.
- Make sure you understand his problem—and he understands yours.
- Help him feel safe. Speak from the heart without exaggerated emotion or anger and always use a nonthreatening tone of voice.
- Don't lose your head in a crisis. Try to remain rational and calm.
- Negotiate (agree to compromise and work on yourself).
- Never underestimate the power of a sincere apology.
- Ask him to read this chapter and agree to practice fair fighting.

14

. . . .

The Big Three: Sex, Commitment, and Marriage

. . . .

As she popped the lid off her soda can, Katie turned and asked, "Anna, how do you deal with sex when you're dating so many guys?"

"Well, when you're engaged . . ." Anna flashed her ring.

There was a long pause before Katie could whisper, "Wow, Anna's off the market."

As Anna threw open her arms to give Katie a big hug, she smiled and replied, "John asked me last night. I was just waiting for the right time to tell you. Now that you're the little date queen yourself, it'll be no time at all till you find someone special, too. Now back to this sex question . . ."

Sex

Before you sleep with someone, know in your mind what it means to you. Ask yourself: What do I expect from this man? Do I care what he's doing when he's not with me? What does this jump into intimacy mean? Will it mean the same thing to him as it does to me? And finally—and the most difficult—is he sleeping with other women? If you don't know the answer, then your relationship is murky, to say the least. He could have another girlfriend or two. Think hard about whether you care or not. If you do, find out what his situation is before you sleep with him. Any sexual relationship should be built on a strong foundation of honesty, whether concerning other current partners or sexual history. Take care of yourself emotionally *and* physically.

When to Have Sex

Although every man I spoke to said that it's perfectly fine to sleep with him on the first date (surprise, surprise), unless you're looking for a purely physical encounter, wait to have sex. It's not because you want to play games, appear hard to get, or reduce him to groveling on his knees. Wait because it gives you time to get to know him and think about what you want and what you're doing before sex gets in the way and impairs your judgment.

In an ideal world, women would deserve the same sexual freedoms men enjoy without judgment. But the reality is that all of us tend to put people into categories. If he thinks you're nonselective or "easy," he may put you in the wrong category and never consider you a "keeper." Give the relationship time to grow; see if it develops into a situation you (and he) are comfortable with. Don't make the mistake in thinking that just because he had sex with you he's going to miraculously wake up and say, "Okay, now I'll get to know her." I know this sounds unfair and that old double standard is rearing its ugly head, but think for a minute—don't you judge men on how promiscuous they are?

On the other hand, physical attraction is an extremely important part of a relationship. Don't write him off till you've checked the chemistry between you: "I've had dinner with him three times, I think he's good-looking and interesting, but there's just no chemistry." Wrong! You can't know for sure until you've kissed him. Chemistry can surprise you. Unshackle Miss Prissy. If you like him, kiss him good night. Give it a try. What do you have to lose? You might just get the surprise of your life. It's only a kiss—what fun you might be missing! But be careful, this is a fine line—don't get yourself into a bad situation and don't be a tease. Keep it light until it's right.

Let's face it, we kid ourselves about our own desires. Say

you go on a few dates, you want to have sex, you do, and it's great. The fact that it *was* great often blurs the rest of the picture. Sometimes, we can't justify or admit to ourselves that we just want a fling. So we convince ourselves that we're in love. We confuse our sexual needs with our emotional needs, which is why we end up wondering how to get out of a two-year relationship that should only have lasted several months. Great sex can be exciting and magical, but it doesn't mean that he will fall in love with you or be the person you need or want for the long-term. Get in touch with your own motivations for getting involved, and don't confuse sex with love.

If you believe that this man is a PFH, then the objective is to get to know him intellectually and emotionally before you get to know him physically. What is his character? How does he feel about all the issues that are important to you? When you develop a strong friendship, before you become sexually intimate, you're more likely to achieve the heightened emotional intimacy that goes hand in hand with a truly wonderful sexual connection. Love—not sex—should be the lure and the glue.

And While We're on the Subject . . .

Your Attitude   Sex starts with you, your attitude toward it and what's going on in your head. Do you feel sexy? Do you see yourself and your body as sexy? If you think sex is boring, scary, or embarrassing, then it will be. You'll find that "headache" will magically disappear when you discover your own body and sexuality. It can be difficult: upbringing or past experiences can inhibit us. So give yourself permission to think about sex in a good, healthy way. Only when you have given yourself this gift will you be able to share it with him.

Enjoy Yourself   Women have been suppressing their sexuality for centuries. Society, religion, and very often our parents have all programmed us to believe that good girls don't enjoy sex. It's time to explode this myth. It is not wrong to enjoy sex. Get those bad-girl images out of your head. Allow yourself to be uninhibited, open-minded, active, and accepting of sex and how it makes you feel.

Communication in Bed Most men want to know what makes you feel good. Any man too proud to learn or too insensitive to care is waving a red flag. If he gets upset when you gently tell him or show him what you like, or if he seems uninterested, he may think he knows it all. If he shows no concern for your emotional and physical well-being, this inflexibility and insensitivity will eventually spill into all aspects of your relationship. If he's a control freak in bed, he isn't looking for an equal relationship or one in which both partners nurture and grow with each other. Show him how to please you but be careful. Sexual prowess or lack of it is a very sensitive subject for everyone. Be gentle—don't criticize him, encourage him.

A giving lover wants to please you. Richie, heartbreaker extraordinaire, had this to say. "I get excited when she gets excited. I want the woman to let herself go." Almost all of the men I interviewed said they wished women would express what pleases them. Richie continues, "I don't want to fumble around in the dark playing guessing games." What if you're not sure what rocks your socks? Then experiment. Learn what pleases you. If you don't know, how can you explain it to him?

Ask yourself what you can do to please him. Everyone is different, and anyone who thinks they're an expert is a fool. Being good in bed is not a generic skill which, once mastered, applies to every partner. Expertise comes from communication and awareness; it's about being able to sense and respond to his needs and desires while making your own preferences known. Tell him you're going to help him learn everything about your body and then give it to him as a gift.

He needs to engage your mind and your body at the same time. Otherwise, sex will just become something you participate in, rather than something that the two of you share. If his focus seems to be only on the act itself, tell him that you like it when he takes his time and teases you. Tell him how excited you get when he talks to you and tells you how much he wants you. But don't turn the bedroom into a school room. Most of all, remember that sex is supposed to be wonderful and fun.

Commitment

You: Deciding to Commit

The day will come when you decide which of these men you want for a serious relationship. Only you can gauge exactly when this will happen. But you should be certain that (a) he is ready for a committed relationship; (b) he has told you in no uncertain terms that he would like to have a serious, committed relationship with you; (c) he has no unbearable personality flaws; and (d) he possesses the must-have character traits on your list.

Relationships always require trust and an initial leap of faith. Just make sure it's an educated leap.

Him: His Freedom

Many men are afraid of a serious commitment or marriage because they feel they'll lose their freedom. Eric, a twenty-six-year-old account executive, told me, "I want to be in control of my own destiny. I don't want any women to tell me I can't watch football or see certain friends. I'm afraid marriage will suffocate me." Instead of resenting him for watching the game on Sunday, use this time to get chores done or visit with your friends. The more freedom a man has in a relationship to be himself, to pursue his dreams, and to live his life, the better chance he'll see that relationship as an enhancement to his life rather than as a threat. Greg, a thirty-eight-year-old veterinarian, agreed wholeheartedly. "If I turn down a sexual offer from another woman out of fear or guilt, I'll feel trapped or denied. But, if I turn her down because I feel great about my relationship and don't want to risk losing my girlfriend, then I'll feel positive. I'll feel in control." Craig, a twenty-nine-year-old airline pilot, had this to say: "As soon as a woman starts telling me what I can or cannot do, I shut down. I feel like I'm sixteen and being lectured by my parents. I immediately become resentful and usually rebel out of spite."

Ian had gone through a messy divorce in his early twenties and was reluctant to make another marriage mistake. His current girlfriend of four years, Isabelle, knew he loved her, yet was painfully aware of his fear of commitment. So she decided to give him breathing room and pursue her life goal of finally getting her college degree. Though it took her three years to complete and took her six hundred miles away, she felt wonderful and proud of her accomplishment. Ian finally proposed. He adores the amazing, independent, and secure woman she proved herself to be. Isabelle's unavailability didn't stem from playing hard to get but from a desire for self-fulfillment and an enriched life.

In the best relationship, there is implicit trust. You trust him to choose his own experiences because they will be consistent with his respect for himself and the relationship. And yes, some men abuse this trust, expecting no boundaries. In this case, there's a limit to how much freedom is reasonable.

Both of You: Commitment = Work

Some women equate marriage with complete and utter bliss. In reality it requires constant attention and work. Think about it. Aside from having a child, marriage is the most serious commitment you can make. Yet how often have you worked harder at your job than your relationship? We expend so much energy maintaining other things in our lives, why do we think we can get away with putting our relationships on automatic pilot? Great relationships don't happen. They take work.

However—and this is essential—look for someone with this same mind-set. It doesn't matter if you're incredibly compatible or completely in love. If he won't work at the relationship, it's doomed. It takes two to care.

Moving In

Once you're in a serious, committed relationship, you may find yourself spending more time at his place than your own. You may think about moving in together. When you're frustrated because half your clothes are across town, and you're thinking that one rent would be cheaper than two, resist the temptation of living together for convenience's sake. If you want marriage, keep your own place until you're engaged and have a date set or are married. If you've followed the program so far and have cultivated a healthy frame of mind about men and relationships, it's unlikely you'll be wanting to move in too soon. This is in contrast to a woman without a strong foundation and multiple sources of fulfillment, who will eagerly seek to mesh herself in her boyfriend's space.

Sarah, a girlfriend from college, moved in with her boyfriend of two years, Frank, hoping this would expedite a serious commitment. But the focus quickly shifted from the relationship to the excitement of "playing house." A year and a half later Sarah was surprised and devastated to hear that he wanted to break up. In retrospect they realized that the relationship had stopped growing soon after they moved in together. Frank's motivation diminished, because he was now concentrating on his leisure activities rather than cultivating a deep connection. Sarah was equally guilty, as she had been focusing on the home and the details of living together. Unless a strong base of compatibility and commitment is already formed, moving in prematurely will only hurt your chances of marriage.

Evading Monotony

As we grow with a relationship, overwhelmed by day-to-day practicalities, we forget to tell and show our partner that we love him. Once you're in a long-term relationship, don't let it become routine. If you stop looking for adventure in life, you lose your spark. And partners who take each other for granted lose the very connection that brought them together and made their relationship so special. Don't let the romance die just because you're no longer caught up in the excitement of dating. How can you do it? Make time to nurture and appreciate each other.

Think of ways to add spice and variety to your lives. Karen and Michael, for example, started ballroom dancing. It infused their relationship with passion, energy, and romance. Tom and Lisa have an understanding that every week, they take turns planning a special surprise date for each other. They think of things to do and places to go that their partner would enjoy. For example, Tom once surprised Lisa, a budding entrepreneur, with tickets to the hot Broadway show *How to Succeed in Business Without Really Trying*. She reciprocated with tickets to hear his favorite comedian.

The Rush for Marriage

"I never married, because there was no need. I have three pets at home which answer the same purpose as a husband. I have a dog which growls every morning, a parrot which swears all afternoon, and a cat that comes home late at night."—Marie Corelli

The "M" Word

Before we talk about marriage, let me just say one thing: Enjoy the Journey! Make your relationship a joyful, positive experience. Promise yourself you'll enjoy it day to day. Remember, nobody knows what the future holds or where the relationship can lead. So focus your energy and attention on having fun and learning as you go. When you continually plan, control, and rush the relationship, you prevent joy from manifesting. Allow it to grow naturally. By taking time to enjoy each other now, you're laying the foundation for a strong, healthy, and long-lasting future.

The Spinster Trap

The despair that you may never marry can send you running into the arms of unhappiness, unfulfillment, and Mr. Wrong (or it may send Mr. Right running in the other direction). Wipe this idea out of your head. You are not desperate now, and you never will be. You may feel sad or lonely, but marriage to the wrong person won't solve those problems, and a man won't make you feel whole.

Too many women rush into marriage because they think it will save them from loneliness, financial responsibilities, or their family. But only you can save yourself by fighting to make your own life better. Not only do these challenges build character, but you'll learn how to be independent and make yourself happy. After all, the day may come when neither your parents, friends, or a man will be there to take care of you and you'll have to take care of yourself. It's best to learn now.

If you've never been very independent, then ask yourself how you can start to take on more responsibility. For instance, learn to balance your own checkbook. Many of us cringe at adding more responsibility to our lives. Yet this is exactly what we all need to do to be independent. We must develop ourselves and be content with our own lives before merging it with someone else's. A man is an added bonus to your own success. He's the frosting, but you're the cake.

Settling Down Doesn't Mean "Settling"

Many women are in a big hurry to settle down and have kids. They operate on a preconceived timetable, either their own or someone else's. They forget there is a big difference between "settling" and "settling down." People who settle say, "He seems good enough. I'm not really happy, but I probably won't find anyone else." *A decision made in desperation is the wrong one.*

Some women are convinced that they can make it work. They hope, somehow, to change a man or the chemistry and dynamics of the relationship. Nine times out of ten, though, this attitude leads to frustration, unhappiness, and relationships that crash and burn.

You should never succumb to outside pressure. Well-meaning family, friends, and coworkers don't realize the stress they create by questions such as, "So what's going on? Is he the one? Has he popped the question?" This kind of pressure can play with your head. Instead, relish your time and stay in the present. Think to yourself, "This is fun. I enjoy seeing him, but I need time to make sure I really want him."

Desperation Is Ugly

How do desperate women come across to men? Men think to themselves "This woman is a burden and I will end up having to take care of her. She is high emotional maintenance. I don't think I can have a balanced, pressure-free relationship with her." Dorothy, thirty-four, a very pretty, successful doctor, loses herself in love every time she dates. She makes his world her own. She drops her interests and her friends for his, rarely makes a decision for herself, and starts looking at wedding dresses. Through the years, I've known three guys who dated Dorothy. They all confided in me that they quickly felt overwhelmed by feeling solely responsible for Dorothy's happiness. As Dorothy gave up her interests and independence for each new man, she stopped making *herself* happy. As my friend Steve, a thirty-nine-year-old partner at a law firm, explained, "It's like she was a strangling, clinging vine that started around my ankle and slowly worked her way up to my neck. That's when I went out and bought a gallon of weed-be-gone."

Men have enough problems of their own. They don't want more. Instead, they want a partner who's easygoing and gives them freedom to carry on their own friendships, jobs, and activities. Men love someone who can add to their life. Men don't want a needy woman, but rather a woman who has her own life! Relationships and marriage are the union of two, not the elimination of one.

The Biological Clock

One big source for a sense of desperation is the ticking biological clock. Women start to think, "I have to get married *now*, before it's too late to have children." Unfortunately, many settle for the wrong person, making their lives miserable. Not only are they in a loveless, noncompatible relationship, but they've dragged children into the mess.

Ultimately, it's self-destructive to have children in a loveless marriage. You won't be happy, and neither will your children. Have foresight. It's much better to wait for a man you truly love than to marry a man who happens to be available.

I am not denying the unfortunate reality that as we age, it's harder to have children. Although the obvious ideal is for children to be brought up by both parents, if your motherly instincts are too overwhelming to ignore, there are options you can choose while you're searching for your soul mate. These include adoption, artificial insemination, freezing embryos, and working with underprivileged children. Times are changing. If you have a supportive extended family nearby and are financially secure, single parenthood can be a valid choice. Actress Michelle Pfeiffer adopted a child on her own and met her true soul mate two months later. So you never know.*

If you're thinking about motherhood but Mr. Right is still nowhere in sight and you know you want a child one day, one pathway is to learn more about IVF, a process where eggs or embryos are harvested and frozen until you're ready to have children.† This option may offer you great peace of mind.

Other Age Issues

Our society is very youth-oriented, and many men do care about your age. Sad but true. It's one of the first questions many men want to know. If children are part of his future

---

*For more information pick up a copy of *Single Mothers by Choice* by Jane Mattes.
†To find out more about this procedure, contact Dr. Jerome Check, Medical Director of the Cooper Center for IVF in Marlton, N.J., or your nearest IVF clinic.

plans, he may be doing the standard calculation: one year to get to know her, plus a few years of being married before kids, equals she's too old, so no chance for her! Or he may think, "She's too young to be taken seriously." It isn't fair that men make these judgments, but they do. And in a way, we do, too. So how do you respond to that question?

I know I've been promoting honest communication, but in this case if you tell the truth, you risk rejection. Yet if you evade the truth, you face eventual discovery and possibly his loss of trust. On the other hand, most of the men I spoke to said that if they didn't know a woman's age and fell for her, they'd be willing to compromise. What a Catch-22. If you think a promising relationship is threatened by your age, you can choose to evade the answer at first. It gives him a chance to get to know you unencumbered by prejudices. Here are some lighthearted responses: "I've never been good with numbers; my accountant handles that." "Why? Do you put an age limit on friendship?" Or, "Old enough to know better and young enough to do it again." "I'm ageless and timeless and I feel great." "How old do you want me to be?" "I believe you're as old as you think and feel." Or, "Don't you know you're never supposed to ask a woman her age or if her jewels are real?" "We shouldn't judge each other on age." "How old do you think I am? Wow, good guess." The danger in this approach lies in the moment when evasiveness becomes a lie. When or if that occurs—and how much it could damage the relationship— is a highly individual matter. It depends on your conscience, the man, the reason for the age question, and where you are in the relationship. Luckily, some men don't make it an issue.

Talking About It/The Proposal

You have to be careful when talking about marriage. Even if you're only speaking hypothetically, many men take the mere mention of the "M" word as a proposition or a death threat! However, when they talk to you about marriage, it can be a proposal of sorts. Many men like to test the waters first—after all, no man wants to be rejected when he pops the question. He wants to be the one to propose once he's decided that he's ready, the time is right, and that you're the one. If this just doesn't work for you, you always have the option of expressing your love and asking for a commitment, commonly known to men as the "ultimatum." Proceed with caution. You'll get an answer, but be prepared that it may not be the one you're looking for. You may lose him and wish you'd just enjoyed your time with him rather than pushing the marriage issue before he was ready. Or you might learn that commitment will never be in the cards and decide it's time to cut him loose.

However, there *are* things you can do to encourage his proposal. After you've thought realistically about what life would be like with him, and you know you're right for each other, try showing in words and actions how important he is to you. "Honey, you're the greatest man in the world, I hope we're always together." Be his biggest supporter, his best friend. Give yourself freely, focus on enjoying the time you spend together, and let him come to you willingly. Don't force the issue. He'll appreciate you rather than resent you.

A Word of Warning

Many women think that marriage is the ultimate goal. Some are so relieved when a man proposes that they accept without thinking whether they'd be happy married to him. Remember, he may have asked the magic question and chosen a sparkling ring, but he's still the same man. Any issues or problems you have won't suddenly resolve themselves. As any wise, experienced woman would tell you, marriage is not a tonic. If anything, issues become more intense as your lives become entwined. Use this time now to make sure you both can work things out.

Remember

- Before you sleep with him, ask yourself if this jump in intimacy will mean the same thing to him as it does to you.

- Commitment does not equal control. Let him run his own life.
- The more freedom you give him, the more he'll want to be with you.
- Marriage or a man won't make you whole.
- Be content with your own life before you merge it with someone else's.
- When you stop desperately looking for a man and focus your attention on *your* life and accomplishments, you'll find yourself and, most likely, the right partner.
- Don't succumb to outside pressure; make your own decisions.
- Replace desperation with self-respect.
- If you're not happy with the relationship *before* children, you won't be happy *after* them.
- To reap the rewards of a healthy, committed relationship you need to work at it every day.

15

....

Be a Survivor

....

She still couldn't believe Anna was getting married, and now Louise was single. Poor Lou, Katie thought as she remembered her teary-eyed call. "The only thing I could get out of him was that he wishes I were more independent. I don't understand," sobbed Louise. "I eat dinner with you guys at least every three weeks, and I never complain when he's out with his friends." Katie wondered if Lou was ready to hear that going out with the girls every three weeks was hardly giving him breathing space.

When a Relationship Ends

Every human being has the freedom to change at any instant.

—Victor Frankl

After every miniheartbreak, my younger sister Flora and I used to remind each other, "Men are like buses: there'll be another along in fifteen minutes, so don't cry for any longer than that." Unfortunately, all too often we feel as if the bus has run us over and the driver isn't even slowing down to inspect the damage.

Love is great: There's nothing better. But the end of a relationship can be one of the most painful things you'll ever endure. Few things in life can hurt us more deeply. The pain can feel crippling. Every time you think or talk about it, you revisit the pain, your stomach ties itself up in knots, and you feel physically and emotionally sick. Even a year later, the thought of bumping into your ex-lover's friends—or, God forbid, him—can send you into a tailspin. As you suffer through the agony of love withdrawal, you're forced to come face-to-face with yourself: your flaws and fears. Confronted with this, it's easy to wonder if you have the strength to go on. Recovering is one of the hardest things you'll ever have to do.

If you open up your heart, no matter how careful you are, you risk suffering hurt and disappointment. You can, however, minimize the anger, pain, self-consciousness, and time spent in "the pit" after a breakup. You can survive. And you can do more than survive, you can use this time to develop greater self-awareness. Relationships enlighten us, giving us vital information through positive and negative feedback to help us make healthier choices in the future. Any difficulty in a relationship is an opportunity to examine yourself and how your attitudes, moods, beliefs, and behaviors might have contributed to the situation.

When broken and damaged, repair is necessary. Each of us has to find our own path through the pain. Some women immerse themselves in work, some move to a different city, others buy a new wardrobe. There are things you can do—not to cure yourself (only time can do that), but to make it less painful and to minimize the negative impact on your life.

When you're in the pit of despair and you can't find your way out, here are my fifteen steps to survival. They have helped me, and I hope they'll help you.

Let Him Go

If he comes back of his own volition, his commitment will be stronger. But if you try to force or trick him into coming back, you'll only hurt yourself. Calling him or writing him letters is deluding yourself that he'll magically come back. It's a form of self-inflicted torture. Some women keep in touch with

his friends or family in the hopes of keeping their lives en-
meshed. One of my girlfriends went so far as to leave a pump-
kin at her ex's doorstep as a Halloween present so he'd call her.
Another girlfriend heard her ex was hosting a dinner party.
She set out across town to his neighborhood to see whose cars
were in his driveway. As she was slowly rounding the bend
opposite his house, checking out the action rather than the
road, she sideswiped an incoming party guest's car, causing a
loud noise and much commotion. Her astonished ex-beau, his
neighbors, and the party guests came out to see what happened. Imagine how embarrassed she was when she was
caught in her "drive-by" sleuthing. Remember, every time you
see or talk to him, it takes you another three weeks to get him
out of your system. There is a lot to be said for just staying away.

At this point, you're probably very angry at him, but this
pent-up rage and resentment needs to be released. Negativity,
anger, and bitterness eat away at your soul. Purge yourself by
making a list of all the ways he hurt you. Spend a day being
angry, very angry. Close your eyes and imagine a nice long
boxing match. Go down each issue one by one and let him
have it till he's out cold. By releasing all the things that made
you angry, your heart can start to heal and you'll be able to
move forward emotionally and someday love again. In contrast some women keep themselves in pain by obsessing over
their loss, thinking again about the first kiss or the well-
planned birthday surprise. "He was so gorgeous, affectionate,
supportive . . . I'll never find anyone comparable."

No space can be filled until it has been emptied. When you
have the courage to leave a space open, the opportunity exists
for it to be filled with something or someone wonderful and
completely new. Remember, you can't make him want you or
love you. If your ex doesn't want you as much as you want
him, he's not your soul mate. It's not meant to be. Why not
make room for someone else who can love you as you deserve
to be loved?

Give Yourself Permission to Grieve

Don't be afraid of feeling sadness, anger, fear, and even love. Many women think if they suppress their feelings and keep a stiff upper lip, life will go on and they'll be fine. But you need to *feel* the whole depth of your emotions, so let them pass through like a breeze. If you try to block them rather than opening the floodgates, they'll linger inside of you for years. Before you can erase him from your life and create a happier future you'll need to work through the pain and sadness. It's healthy and normal to mourn. Take your time and don't move on until you're ready.

Women have a tendency to go into solitary confinement at this time. Instead, use love and support to lessen the pain. Rely on your friends and family, people who will let you cry your eyes out and then drag you out for brunch, a jog, or a movie. Lean on them. Friends can provide a loving context in which you can express your sadness. It's important to know that at least one person, be it your mother, sister, or best friend, really loves you and empathizes deeply with your pain. It's still going to be a rough time, but knowing that someone's there to help you through can make all the difference.

Let those who love you know, "This is a very bad time for me. I am deeply sad, and I'd really welcome your support." Let them know and then allow them to help you. They'll make the difference between slow, painful change and a quick recovery. If you feel like crying, call one of your friends. Don't think you're bothering her; you'll be closer because you have shared a real, emotional heart-to-heart talk. Every good cry has a cleansing effect helping to purge the pain. Let them know you appreciate their help and guidance.

But as you begin to rely on your support network, remember that everyone has their own stresses, challenges, and time constraints. When we most need our friends to be there is often when we feel them evaporate. This can be for several reasons. Our problems may seem overwhelming—they know they can't solve them and are afraid to open a Pandora's box.

Or they may want to help but have no clue how. Or they may be afraid of pain and suffering and don't want to somehow jinx their own life and relationships. Make it easy for your friends by isolating one or two problems for them to help you with. Clarifying for yourself what you need makes it easier for others to give.

Own Your Feelings

Don't blame your parents, friends, boss, or ex for the way you feel. They are your feelings and your problems, and you need to work them out. Being aware of how this breakup affects you and gaining insight into your own behavior patterns are positive moves toward getting you out of the pit. Feeling like a victim isn't. When you let a man or others make you feel badly about yourself, you're giving up your power. Why let others make you depressed? Recognize that they're not making you feel unhappy, you're allowing yourself to feel this way. You have the power to make yourself feel better. You're in control. You have a choice, in every moment, of whether you'll stay open to your love and spirit or contract and close down in pain.

Face the things that are interfering with getting and keeping love in your life. These are the things that make you feel uncomfortable or scared. It's much easier to deal with the truth than to spend all of your energy resisting it.

Remind Yourself: The Only Person You Can Control Is Yourself

The only thing you can control is your own behavior. You can't choose how other people treat you, but you can choose to conduct yourself in a certain manner. And that's what matters. You control how you react to the people who hurt, disappoint, or reject you. If you are who you say you are, then a man's hurtful words or actions will not change your character. You control who you choose to be. You're a valuable person, whether he's with you or not. So don't let his bad behavior shut you down or change who you are. The times when you're at your lowest are when you especially need to remember who you are. It's not about what he is or isn't doing, saying, or being. Don't let him change you into a weak, withdrawn, sad creature. Your intrinsic value remains the same, no matter how others treat you.

If you have reached out in love and continue to come from a place of love, then whatever he says, however he responds, is inconsequential. You have given your best. The fact that it's not good enough is further proof that it's time to move on!

You chose to take the risk and go into the relationship, and some good and some bad came out of it. Now is the time to take stock of your life choices and choose to do something else.

Don't Personalize

"If I were only ten pounds lighter or younger or blonder, then maybe he would have stayed." Does this sound familiar? Banish these thoughts. They give him control. Stop asking yourself why the breakup occurred, if it was your fault, or if you were good enough. You forgot to take into account that he was only twenty-four and not ready to settle down, or that his parents would have disowned him if he'd married a *shiksa*, or that he wasn't sure about his own heterosexuality, or maybe he was just a jerk! To be a survivor, you have to make a conscious effort to not put yourself down. This means *stop blaming yourself!*

You must stop all of the negative voices. Every time you hear them, stop and replace them with a new positive voice: Yes, I am good enough! Yes, I look fine! Keep repeating the positives. Vow to notice each time the negatives come up and reverse and replace them with positives.

Love Yourself

After we lose the one we love, we often stop loving ourselves. Instead of letting our family and friends move into that empty space, we find ourselves more alone, wondering, "Who really loves me?" It's now that we need to be reminded that we love *ourselves*. Don't desert yourself when you're needed most. Be your own cheerleader. When the voice inside whispers that you're alone, that nobody really loves you, tell it strongly that you are there. Look in the mirror and repeat over and over that you are loved and you can conquer anything! Fight for yourself, don't just lie down and let the negative voices win. It's within you to find the courage and strength to move forward step by step.

Take time out for yourself. You deserve it. One of my girlfriends fluctuates between Club Med and checking into a spa after every big breakup. She emerges looking and feeling much better. Treat yourself to bubble baths by candlelight, a massage, a new outfit, a new haircut. Spoil yourself, splurge, buy yourself flowers, wear your favorite perfume, make your favorite meal, watch the sun set, or drink hot chocolate and read an inspiring book. Rent all the movies he never wanted to watch with you! *Get to the gym!* The endorphins will help jump-start your system, and you'll look and feel better. Meditation or yoga can help you escape from the chaos and find your center again. Find the time to focus on giving to yourself and making yourself stronger. When you're empowered and full of vigor, it's much easier to move your life forward.

This isn't the time to be overwhelmed by adding more stress. Instead, you need to simplify and declutter your life. Exercise, get enough sleep, spend time with your family, your friends, and your cat. You need to concentrate on rebuilding the foundations of your life, at the center of which is your own self-worth. By quieting down instead of looking for distractions, you'll access the calm and self-assurance that is at your core.

Focus on the Work and People You Love

Have a purpose. Let working on your own dreams and goals replace the time you used to spend focusing on him. My grandmother told me that when her husband of fifty-nine years died, she asked herself what she had to live for. On her own now for seventeen happy years, she recently remarked, "I have so many things to do, and I just don't feel that I have enough time to do them all." If a ninety-two-year-old woman can have this attitude, so can you!

Suffering is a part of any rich, full life. What helps us survive the bad times is knowing that we have created meaning. Family, career, friendships, hobbies, the people we love—all of these help us build purpose. Give the things that mean something in your life more power than your suffering.

It is also important to be fully committed to those you love when they go through difficulties of their own. They need you to tell them, "I know this is a terrible time for you. I'm here for you one hundred percent. I'm not going to let you go through this alone. I love you. We're going to figure out a way to solve this problem together." If you say this and can convince them that you mean it, so much of their fear, anxiety, and depression will melt away. This is one of the most important gifts you can give to the people you love. When they emerge from "the pit," you'll stand out as someone they know they can trust. You will be a real friend that they hold dear. We push ourselves so hard to create equity in our material investments, yet the time spent on building human equity gives the greatest returns of all! And remember—most important—actions speak louder than words!

Give Yourself Time

Whether you have come out of your last relationship fighting or broken, give yourself a cooling-off period. When you don't take any downtime, you can find yourself right back in a similar relationship. You need time to reflect and heal before you get back into the swing of things. Expect that it will take time to feel good about yourself and to function well again. Give yourself a month, six months, a year, whatever it takes. Don't be afraid of being on your own. It's time to focus on getting strong within yourself and empowering your own life.

Know that the pain from even the most wounding breakup cures itself in time. No matter how bleak it seems now, remind yourself that eight months from today you'll be enjoying a happy, contented life. The time will come when the caterpillar will emerge from its cocoon as a butterfly.

Adjust Your Attitude

Regardless of your circumstances and what others do, you're ultimately responsible for yourself and your attitude. Even though I could not choose to leave my abusive household as a child and was in every way a victim of circumstances, I could choose my outlook. There are positive lessons even in your greatest trials. There were many for me. I became excellent at reading and understanding strangers. I learned that I could survive anything and still have an optimistic outlook. So can you! It is all just a matter of changing your viewpoint. See each difficulty as an opportunity to grow. How are you going to see the world? How are you going to approach new situations? Is it going to be with a positive or a negative attitude? Will you be happy, thoughtful, and kind—or bitter and filled with thoughts of revenge? Negative thoughts, comments, and actions have a poisonous effect on our heart, mind, and soul, just as smoke has on our lungs. Turning years' or even days' worth of negative thoughts and actions into positive ones can happen in an instant, as we have the power to choose to change at anytime. The results will enrich your life dramatically.

During tough times and breakups, we have a choice. You can defeat yourself and say: I'm a victim. I'll never be happy again. I'm not good enough. He ruined my life. Or you can choose to be a survivor and say I'm going to make it through this. I'm going to get over this, no matter how hard it is. Take ownership of yourself, take on the responsibility and pick survival. If you aren't whole, you can't do all the things you want to do. And you can't be happy until you change your outlook from doom and gloom to "I will survive!"

Look at this wounding experience as a chance to grow,

expand, and develop. Remember, when you jump into the deep end of life, you learn to swim very quickly. Look at adversity as an opportunity to find out what you're made of. Let it empower you to greatness. If you can overcome this, you can do anything. Your attitude will determine how you feel and how others will react to you.

If you want to survive and get through the pain, you have to look at all of your experiences as challenges and all of your challenges as experiences. When everything we have is gone, stripped away by a devastating blow, we're left with just our core. But it's an incredible opportunity to rebuild ourselves to be more self-aware, understanding, and empathetic. Use this time to really look at yourself. Seek counseling, read self-help books, practice meditating, or do anything else that will help you learn, grow, and become a better person. Our soul evolves and strengthens with pain. You've heard it before—it's true—believe it!

Make a List of Solutions

What can you possibly do to get yourself out of this funk? Make a list, of course! List every step you can think of to solve your problems. Imagine obstacles as the rocks on the road. Maneuver around them or march right over them. Also list the simple, everyday things you can do that will make you happier. For example, spend more time with those friends who make you laugh. Learn to play an instrument. Singing, even if you are alone in the shower, is incredibly restorative. Make a tape of your favorite songs. Find time every day while dressing or driving to sing along.

Use Positive Imagery

It's important that while taking steps toward what you want externally you also work internally. Imagining and sensing in your mind and body the outcome you desire can put a part of you in your future, making it only a matter of time before it is fully manifested. President Kennedy used to tell the story about a group of Irish boys who climbed a big fence by taking off their hats first and throwing them over the fence so a part of them was already on the other side. This incentive made the fence easier to climb.

Go to the future in your mind and use the power of this image to help propel you forward. See yourself as already having reached your goal, then look back at where you are now. The very process of focusing clearly on the future unharnesses a creative process that guides you forward toward that destiny.

Whether you're daydreaming or praying, don't idealize the past or imagine that you want your old life and ex-relationship back. Instead, embrace change and visualize and request the best man and life for you. Focus on how much better your life is going to be moving forward. When you're stuck in the past, it's hard to imagine yourself looking back and thanking your lucky stars that you got out of a relationship that wasn't meant to be. Yet this is inevitably what happens. Bask in your new freedom and look forward to the potential of happiness and fulfillment. Create the environment you need for that personal vision to flourish. Be creative. Draw, paint, or write down your feelings in a diary.

Help Others, But Not at the Expense of Yourself

When we hurt, we go into our shell to protect ourselves. We curl up into a ball in the safest place we can find (usually our bed). Our focus is inward, to nurse our wounds and sometimes to feel sorry for ourselves. Try looking outward to others who need a helping hand. No matter how bad you feel, if you look around you will notice others with bigger problems than your own. For a short time, stop concentrating on your own sadness and problems and help someone else. Make yourself useful; volunteer at a soup kitchen, children's hospital, or homeless shelter. Convert the pain and grief you feel into energy to help others. The rewards for being generous with your spirit will be outstanding. No heart is so small or so broken that it doesn't have room to love another. You have learned a lot about pain. Take the time to notice others who are suffering and make the effort to smile and say a kind word. It will help you both.

Always help others in need, but not at the expense of yourself. Some years ago, while I was putting a sibling through drug rehabilitation, a girlfriend of mine was institutionalized with a severe case of manic depression. Their problems soon became my own, as my focus turned to helping them get their lives back on track. Then Josh, an SYT I had rather recklessly fallen in love with, broke my heart. I was so involved with the care of my friends that I could barely take care of myself. Overwhelmed, I quickly plunged into the saddest time of my life. Finally, after heeding another wise friend's advice to just "cut them loose," I told them that I couldn't take care of them anymore. They both became hostile, and I was guilt-ridden. But then, slowly, amazingly, they began to take care of themselves. Other people in their lives began to pitch in, and I was free of an enormous amount of pressure. Some call it "tough love," but sometimes the biggest gift we can give a dependent is the example of taking care of ourselves. I had learned two important lessons, (1) not to burden myself with others' problems to the point where it became a threat to my own well-being and (2) to cherish the strong people in my life who could support me when I was in need.

Enjoy Every Day

You have three choices where you can be: reliving the past, fearful or hopeful with fantasies of the future, or here and now in the present. Find happiness every day. When we are beaten down, sad, and lonely, it's then, more than ever, that we must force ourselves to find and enjoy the beauty in each day. *Don't postpone happiness.* Write this down and put it in a spot where you will see it daily. Keep reminding yourself to look for and appreciate the small things that make you feel happy each day. Don't live in the past, celebrate the present!

Close your eyes and imagine you're taken out of your life

and are now in a small dark cave. Stay in this cave for five minutes. Feel the chill, the loneliness. Back in reality, there's much
you can find to be thankful about. Make a list of every single
thing that's good. Look for more every day and add them to
your list.

Push yourself to go out and have fun. If you feel it's the last
thing you want to do, then it's probably what you need to do
most. Attend that party—say yes to the girls' night out. Dress
up so you look and feel like a million bucks. You never know,
you may have fun despite yourself. You may even meet a
CB. (There is no better tonic for a broken heart than a kiss from
a CB.)

Take One Step at a Time

Life can seem overwhelming when taken as a whole.
Don't use this one failure as evidence that your life won't work
out. That's ridiculous. If the despair is overwhelming, concern yourself with just getting through each moment. Break
your problems down to simple steps and attack a small one
every day.

Regain Hope and Faith

As we run around accomplishing our daily activities, we
don't think about faith and hope very much. The incredible
power and importance of these two words only hits us when
we find ourselves without them. Without hope and faith, life is
not worth living. Understanding their importance may one
day save your life or the life of someone very dear.

One of my best friends had once again been left by a man
she thought she was going to marry. In fact, she had put incredible career possibilities on hold just so she could travel
with Mr. Right. When she came to see me, she cried, "I know
I'm never going to find someone to love and have a family
with. My life is never going to work out. I can't take it anymore. I just can't live a life with so much pain. I'd rather be
dead!" It sent shivers through my whole body as I felt her pain

and the absence of any hope or faith. It took some time, but with love, reassurance, and encouragement, my friend has established new hopes for the future. She regained faith. Now, less than one year later, she has started her own successful company, is dating a wonderful man, and is happier than she has been in years.

Remember

By focusing on your attitude, work, family, friends, and what you've learned from this breakup, you can restore the purpose in your life and thereby regain your faith and hope in the endless possibilities the future has to offer. Keep your perspective. There is so much more to your life than one relationship. Have faith that even this has happened for a reason, and let the hope for a better future pull you out of the pit of despair. Life is about new beginnings. Now you really can start fresh. This is your chance to go out and do anything.

Final Message

Katie kicked off her skates, leaned back on the loveseat, and looked out the window. Was it her imagination or was life much more fun? As she reached for the phone, she wondered if Lou had spent enough time recovering. "Lou, do I have plans for us, get ready, I'm taking you out hunting tonight. You'll love it!" She smiled to herself as she remembered her first hunting expedition with Anna months before.

The dating revolution has begun. Now that you know how to screen, meet, and set up dates with the men you choose, you'll never have to wait by the phone or settle again.

We are at the last frontier leading to intimacy and equality between the sexes. It's time for women to change our conditioning and take a proactive approach to all aspects of our lives. Challenge yourself to be the best you can be! Life is an exciting journey full of surprises and changes. Find your purpose and then make each moment count. Start creating the life, job, and friendships you dream of, and get a life *before* you get a man. How do successful people make things happen in their lives? Chances are, they have achieved their goals by:

Developing a life plan
Getting organized
Doing their homework

Believing in themselves
Focusing and setting clear and realistic goals
Taking action; daring to take risks
Surrounding themselves with positive people
Being persistent

This program is the rocket fuel that will propel you into a fulfilling life. Daring to manifest your dreams will unleash your confidence, passion, and power. Trust me—when you radiate a happy, exuberant love for life, heads will not stop turning. No man can wave a magic wand and provide you with a magical life; it's up to you to create an amazing life for yourself. There is nothing more exciting to a man than a confident, independent woman with a life of her own. Allow yourself to shine, and don't let anyone (including yourself) hold you back.

Godspeed and Happy Hunting!

If you would like to contact the author,
share your success stories,
or be put on the mailing list, visit
www.jenniferbawden.com
or write to
Jennifer Bawden
P.O. Box 6086,
Yorkville Station, NY, 10128.
To set up a personal coaching session
please call: 212-876-9000.